Jolly Time

PATRICIA FOX SHEINWOLD

PARTY BOOK

DORISON HOUSE PUBLISHERS, INC.
Cambridge/New York

Copyright © 1977 by Dorison House Publishers, Inc.
Published by Dorison House Publishers, Inc.
Cambridge / New York

ISBN: 0-916752-21-6
Library of Congress Catalog Card Number 77-89553
Manufactured in the United States of America

Acknowledgment
The author gratefully acknowledges the contribution
and cooperation of Anne Halliday.

For Andrew and Jordan

CONTENTS

PREFACE

The makers of Jolly Time Pop Corn take pride and pleasure in presenting this book. They hope you will take pride in decorating your home for the holidays and pleasure in the suggested activities and recipes. The book is designed for the younger members of the family to participate in the planning and execution of the parties instead of standing on the sidelines. Step-by-step instructions are given along with diagrams and illustrations. The games recommended for the parties can be interchanged from one holiday to another. There is even an original tune for musical chairs. There are magic tricks and puzzles and an answer page in case you get stuck. There are card games to tempt your skill and card tricks to tickle your guests. There are homemade gift ideas and how to make them. Jolly Time wants its readers, young and old, to be informed so throughout the book you will find interesting as well as historical facts about pop corn. But best of all, you'll discover the many new uses for pop corn, in and out of the stomach.

In this period of back-to-basics, Jolly Time encourages participation by all in family endeavors. From the writing of your first invitation until the last bit of food has been devoured, they want you to have a jolly time.

INTRODUCTION

First, a story. A real, true-to-life story about pop corn and the people who are responsible for it. It's not only an interesting story but from it children can make an informative report for their school work.

Once upon a time, in 1914, Cloid H. Smith sat in the basement of his home in Sioux City, Iowa, shelling and packaging pop corn by hand. His helper was his son, Howard. Pop corn was a novelty in those days but not to C.H. His family had popped corn on their farm in Sac County, Iowa, the heart of the pop corn country, when he was a boy. Just think —no bags or cans at your fingertips down at the local grocery store. If you found it at all, it was either still on the cob or roughly shelled in bulk, bagged at 150 pounds per, "cracker barrel" style.

As all inventors or beginners in an industry know, success does not come easily nor immediately. C.H. was working for the Odebolt Telephone Company in 1899 but filed away in his memory bank was a statement made in 1885 by George Colton, a New Yorker, who said "The growing conditions in Iowa are ideal for pop corn." It was Mr. Colton who introduced pop corn to the Sac County farmers. As C.H. worked his way up to general manager of the telephone company, his new promotion forced him to move to Sioux City in 1905. The company became a part of a larger system, Bell Telephone, in 1912. Although C.H. stayed with the company, he did sell his stock and with the money purchased some land north of Odebolt.

And now the story unfolds. C.H. had a tenant farmer on his land who raised some pop corn, harvested and sold it to a buyer. C.H. thought the price was too low, so he questioned the buyer. They could not agree and when the buyer confronted C.H. with, "If you don't like the way I do business, why don't you go into the pop corn business yourself?" And that's exactly what C.H. Smith did.

So another American dream, a real success story, began. Fortunately for all the future pop corn eaters, C.H.'s dream included nothing but "quality pop corn." He believed that properly processed and packaged high-quality pop corn could be sold in huge amounts. And to be proper his pop corn would not contain any "old maids": kernels that wouldn't pop open. So he set out to prove he was right. First, he designed storage cribs for his corn. The first crib had a 500,000 pound capacity (probably the first built exclusively for storage and curing) and this did improve the corn's popping quality. The crib dried the corn with natural air ventilation, and properly dried corn meant instant popping and no "old maids." By the end of the first year, 75,000 pounds of pop corn had been sold. His very first sale was a 25-pound shipment to a man in Council Bluffs, Iowa: picked on his Odebolt farm, moved by wagon to their Sioux City home, shelled and cleaned in the basement of his home. By 1915, larger facilities were needed for the shelling and cleaning. They had not only outgrown the basement but also a garage-like shed behind the house, so alongside the new crib another new building was erected. These two buildings were in the town of Leeds, a suburb of Sioux City, and today the same site houses the main processing facilities of the American Pop Corn Company. About this time C.H. resigned from the telephone company as his new business needed his full attention.

Now the Smiths, father and son, had to confront the next problem: how to package the pop corn to insure the consumer of the quality C.H. had promised. The one pound cardboard cartons in use at that time allowed the pop corn to dry out too quickly. The Smiths didn't like that. So, in 1920, they packaged the pop corn in glass jars. The package was airtight but glass was expensive and breakage was high. Mr. Smith took his problem to the American Can Company in Chicago. There a man, Mr. Cadwallader, developed an airtight metal can. We take tin cans for granted but in the early 1920s this was a revolutionary discovery. The can developed for Jolly Time in 1924 was a forerunner of today's beer can. With their new can the Smiths could advertise their product "Guaranteed to Pop."

Besides being found on the grocer's shelf, pop corn was sold by vendors. Almost every town had its local vendors but carnivals and circuses needed vendors, too. Pop corn was being sold every place a crowd gathered. The vendors bought their pop corn in bulk, placed it on their trucks, and would go off to the crowded areas to offer cartons of freshly popped corn. They did quite well as far as profits were concerned and Jolly Time stepped in with a full line of supplies to help them with their sales. The line consisted of corn oil, salt, cartons, and glassine bags. From shelling corn in his basement C.H. Smith was now in the packaging business, in advertising, and in creating a line of related pop corn supplies. His idea had mushroomed into a big business.

Business brings change and one of the major changes in the pop corn business was the color of the corn. Yes, the color. In the 1920s nearly all pop corn grown was of a white variety. Yellow corn was scarce in those days, which made it twice as expensive. Today yellow pop corn is much more plentiful than white. The pop corn machine operators are responsible for making the yellow corn more available. Why? Because there are two major differences between the yellow and the white. First, yellow kernels when popped are larger than the white so the commercial vendors can fill an extra carton or two out of every pound of corn. Secondly, to the eye, the yellow popped corn gives the appearance of being freshly buttered, and all of us will buy the more eye-appealing product.

Meanwhile, back on the Iowa farm, Mr. Smith had to turn his attention to selling his product nationally. This meant a large sales force, backed by national advertising. TV was not around then, so Jolly Time used radio. The printed word was not enough but reinforced with weekly radio broadcasts over several leading stations from coast to coast, Jolly Time became a household word. Americans were short on money and long on time and in the 1930s they were delighted to stay home munching pop corn to General Jolly Time and his Pop Corn Colonels, as the leader and his orchestra were known. Pop corn was and is the cheapest snack. People of the 1970s are as appreciative of this as their fellow snackers were back in the thirties.

At the same time, the electric popper popped on the scene. General Jolly Time made a special offer on the radio, "Send in $1 and Jolly Time will send you an electric popper plus a can of Jolly Time Pop Corn." Can you imagine how many thousands of listeners responded? It was a bargain even for those bleak days.

One of the most frequently asked questions about pop corn is, "Will it pop on the cob?" "No," says Jolly Time and they do speak from experience. In 1931, a fire destroyed a whole crib of corn and there was not one pop!

In 1934, three generations of Smiths attended the 20th anniversary luncheon of the company: C.H. Smith, his son, Howard, and Chesley C. Smith, grandson of C.H., who joined the company in 1941. In 1939, C.H. died but not before his dream had come true. Jolly Time is the giant in the pop corn industry and today, in the 1970s, C.H. Smith's pop corn means quality.

The first family in the White House may mean peanuts, but Jolly Time is the first family of American pop corn.

BIRTHDAY

Everybody loves his birthday
Opening gifts and games to play
Colored candy shared with neighbors
Surprises when you pop the favors

You know how to pop the favors on the birthday table but do you know what makes pop corn pop? Around each kernel of corn there is a thin, hard covering called "enamel." Inside the kernel there is some moisture. When you put pop corn in a pan or popper and turn up the heat the moisture inside turns to steam and expands. When the steam pressure builds up it has nowhere to go. So it explodes and pops—and you have pop corn.

Birthday

IMPORTANT
- Before starting a project, it's a good idea to read through all of the instructions so you will be familiar with the steps and materials required.
- Do not eat the pop corn projects that have been made with toothpicks, pins, sequins, glitter, adhesive tape or glue.
- When working with pop corn or glue, always cover your work surface with waxed paper.
- Some of the projects specify stale pop corn. The reason for this is that stale pop corn will not break as easily as freshly popped corn.
- If pop corn projects are made in advance, cover them to keep off dust and dirt.
- A toothpick is a handy tool for dabbing glue on small areas.
- Always have an experienced cook assist with the cooking.

INVITATION MESSAGE
Time: Fill in the hour, the day and the date.

Place: Write your name, address and ZIP code. Include your apartment number if you live in an apartment building.

R.S.V.P.: This is an abbreviation for a French phrase meaning "please answer." List your phone number here.

CLOWN INVITATION

You will need

Construction paper in assorted colors
Gummed stars
Tracing paper
Thin cardboard
White craft glue
Rubber cement
Black felt-tip pen
Scissors
Pencil
Compass
Envelopes (3 5/8'' x 6 1/2'')

Procedure

1. *Face:* Using a compass, draw a 3'' diameter circle on construction paper. Cut out.

2. *Hat:* Trace hat onto tracing paper. Cut out. Glue to cardboard with rubber cement. When dry, cut hat from cardboard to use as pattern. Lay pattern on a piece of construction paper a different color than face. Trace around edge of pattern with pencil. Cut out. Use pattern again to draw a hat for each face.

3. *Finishing:* Smear white glue on curved edge of hat and press to face as shown. Cut out a 3/4'' diameter circle for nose using same color paper as hat. Glue to center of face. Glue on stars for eyes and draw a big U-shape with black pen for mouth. Paste a few stars to hat as shown.

4. Print BIRTHDAY PARTY on reverse side of hat. Refer to invitation message on p. 13 and fill in party information on back of face.

JOLLY TIME ICE CREAM SANDWICHES
Procedure
1. Follow recipe on p. 120 for making Pop Corn Balls with Molasses Glaze, but instead of making balls, form pop corn into 3'' round patties about 1/2'' thick.
2. Put a scoop of soft (but not melting) ice cream between 2 patties and press together.
3. Put in freezer to firm.
4. Serve in a bowl or on a plate.

HELPFUL HINT
Sometimes parties are too large for the average table. In this case, take a large quilt or double-sized flat sheet and put it on the floor of your family room or largest room. Then spread on top of this a paper table cloth purchased at any variety or drugstore. The table cloth could have a Snoopy, Raggedy Ann, or other motif depending on whether boys or girls or both will be at the party. When the ice cream and cake are gone, simply roll up the paper cloth and discard. What could be easier? (The quilt will keep spills from staining your carpeting.)

POP CORN CLOWN CENTERPIECE

Make a clown for each guest to take home and eat.

You will need

Jolly Time Pop Corn—about 2 cups popped corn for each clown

Ingredients for making Pop Corn Balls with Sugar Glaze on p. 118

Pointed ice cream cones—1 for each clown

Small and large gumdrops in assorted colors

8'' paper doilies—1 for each clown

Styrofoam cups—1 for each clown

Procedure

1. Following recipe, make a 3'' diameter ball for each guest using uncolored syrup. Let balls set until firm.

2. Make a small batch of uncolored syrup to use as glue.

3. *Face:* Cut off *flat end* of 3 small gumdrops. Glue small circles to ball with sugar glue to make eyes and nose. Cut off *flat end* of one large gumdrop and cut U-shape out of circle for mouth. Glue in place.

4. *Ears:* Glue a large gumdrop to each side of head. Insert a toothpick through top of gum drop to hold gumdrop to head while glue dries. *Remove toothpicks after glue has set.*

5. *Hat:* Cut off *rounded end* of 3 small gumdrops and glue circles in a row to ice cream cone. Smear a generous amount of sugar glue around rim of cone. Gently press cone to top of head and hold in place until glue sticks.

6. *Collar:* Fold doily in half, fold in half again, then in half once more. Unfold. Gather up center of doily and twist paper at center into a 1'' stem. Spread out edges to form ruffle.

7. *Stand:* Cut off top 2'' of styrofoam cup to form a ring. Place doily on ring, then place clown on top of doily.

8. Set clowns on stands in circle at center of table.

POP CORN POPPER

These are for your guests to take home and eat. The usual paper poppers wind up in the trash can, these wind up in your tummy!

You will need

Jolly Time Pop Corn—about 2 cups popped corn for each popper

Ingredients for making Pop Corn Balls with Molasses Glaze on p. 120

Colored cellophane paper, foil wrapping paper or crepe paper

Curling ribbon

Cellophane tape

Scissors

Procedure

1. Follow recipe for making pop corn balls, but instead of making balls, mold pop corn into cylinders 6'' long x 1 1/2'' diameter.

2. For each cylinder, cut a 12'' square of cellophane paper, foil paper or crepe paper. After cylinders are firm, roll up each cylinder in the center of each square. Hold with cellophane tape. (If cylinders are to be wrapped with crepe paper, cover cylinder first with clear plastic wrap.)

3. Cut 6 14'' pieces of curling ribbon for each popper. Gather up paper at each end of cylinder. Holding 3 pieces of ribbon together, tie center of ribbons around gathered ends and knot securely. Curl ribbons with edge of scissors. If you like, you can cut the ends of the paper to make fringe.

4. Set a popper at each place setting as a favor for your guests to take home and eat.

POP CORN BIRTHDAY CAKE

You will need

Jolly Time Pop Corn—3 1/2 quarts popped corn
Ingredients for making Pop Corn Balls with Molasses Glaze on p. 120
Two 9'' x 1 1/2'' layer cake pans
10 1/2-ounces miniature marshmallows
Small gumdrops in assorted colors
Cake candles
Waxed paper
Double boiler

Cake layers

Follow recipe for making Pop Corn Balls with Molasses Glaze, but instead of making balls press

glazed pop corn into 2 greased layer cake pans. After pop corn has set 5 minutes, unmold onto waxed paper by pressing your thumbs against bottom of pans.

Marshmallow icing

Place miniature marshmallows in top of double boiler with 3 tablespoons of water. Cook until they have melted into a creamy consistency. Stir occasionally. Spread 1/3 of the icing on one of the pop corn layers. Set second layer on top. Spread rest of icing over top of cake and let excess icing drip down sides.

Decoration

• *Note:* Place a small bowl of water next to your working area. Dip knife and fingers into water as you work to keep gumdrops from sticking.

1. Cut gumdrops of different colors into small pieces. Print name of birthday child across center of cake using the small pieces of gumdrops. Form each letter with a different color.

2. Use whole gumdrops as candle holders. Press point of paring knife 1/8'' into top of gumdrop twice, making a cross. Press candle into center of cross.

3. Set gumdrops with candles around edge of cake.

NAPKIN RING

You will need

Flat, hard candies wrapped in cellophane
Cellophane tape
Paper napkins

Procedure

1. For each napkin ring, cut a 6'' piece of cellophane tape.

2. Press wrapped candies to tape placing candies close together.

3. Overlap ends of tape 1/2'' to form a ring.

4. Unfold napkin. Holding napkin at center, draw half way through ring.

PARTY BASKET PLACE HOLDER

You will need

Jolly Time Pop Corn—about 1/2 cup salted, pop-
ped corn for each basket
Styrofoam beverage cups—1 for each basket
Curling ribbon
Colored pipe cleaners in 9'' lengths—1 for each
basket
Gummed stars
White paper
Black felt-tip pen
Cellophane tape
White craft glue
Scissors

Procedure

1. Cut 1'' off the top of each cup using a sharp
   kitchen knife with a thin blade. Let a parent
   help with the cutting.

2. Handle: Press a pipe cleaner 1'' into cup 1/2''
   below top edge. Fold both ends up and twist
   short end around long end. Attach other end of
   pipe cleaner to opposite side of cup the same
   way.

3. Cut four 10'' pieces of curling ribbon for each
   basket. Holding 2 ribbons together, tie center
   of ribbons to each side of handle. Curl ribbon
   with edge of scissors.

4. Using toothpick, dab glue on stars and paste to
   cups in scattered arrangement. (The glue on
   the back of the stars is not strong enough to
   stick to styrofoam.)

5. Cut 1 1/2'' square from white paper. Print name
   along one edge. Fold opposite edge 1/2'' to
   wrong side. Place fold around handle and hold
   in place with cellophane tape.

6. Fill baskets to the brim with pop corn.

PARTY HAT

You will need
Crepe paper
Curling ribbon
Gummed stars
Cellophane tape
Stapler
Scissors

Procedure

1. For each hat, cut a rectangle 14'' wide x 22'' long from crepe paper.

2. Turn up 2 1/2'' on one long edge to make cuff.

3. Overlap short ends 1'' to form a tube. Hold with cellophane tape. Place 2 staples at overlap on cuff so hat won't come apart when worn.

4. Fold tube flat. On edge opposite cuff, make cuts 2'' deep spaced 3/8'' apart to form fringe.

5. Cut four 14'' pieces of curling ribbon for each hat. Gather up fringed edge of hat. Holding the 4 pieces of ribbon together, tie center of ribbons around base of fringe in a secure knot. Curl ribbon with edge of scissors.

6. Fringe top edge of cuff making cuts 1'' deep spaced 3/8'' apart.

7. Paste stars on cuff in a scattered arrangement.

Birthday Games

BIRTHDAY BROAD JUMP

This game can be played by teams or individuals.

1. Place two 4' pieces of string parallel on the ground or floor about 12'' apart.

2. Have players line up and take turns one at a time.

3. With feet together, players jump over the 2 strings. Any player who lands on or between the strings is eliminated.

4. After all players have taken a turn, move the strings farther apart to make the jump more difficult.

5. Remaining players jump again.

6. Keep moving the string farther apart. The last player left is the winner.

7. Remember to keep your feet together when jumping.

BIRTHDAY COOK

1. Make a circle with chairs.

2. Each player is seated except the birthday child, who stands in the middle of the circle.

3. The birthday child has a big, wooden cooking spoon and is the "Birthday Cook."

4. Birthday Cook starts with these words, "Stir and stir the birthday cake. Stir and stir..." Suddenly the cook drops the spoon.

5. When the spoon is dropped this is the signal for everyone to change chairs. Cook races for empty chair.

6. The player left standing becomes the next cook.

BIRTHDAY WORDS

1. Each player gets pencil and paper and writes his name at top of paper.

2. Have players write the word BIRTHDAY in 2 columns. One column goes up and the other column goes down as shown.

B	Y
I	A
R	D
T	H
H	T
D	R
A	I
Y	B

3. The object of the game is to make as many words as you can by starting a word with a letter in the first column and ending the word with the corresponding letter in the second column. For example:

B	Y	boy
I	A	idea
R	D	read
T	H	tenth

4. In other words, the first word must start with a B and end with a Y. The second word starts with an I and ends with an A. You can put as many letters in the middle as you wish.

5. Try to make as many words as you can. Sometimes you can't think of a word, so just go on to the next set of letters.

6. The winner is the player who has made the most words.

7. In case of a tie, the player who uses the longest words is the winner.

8. Set a time limit.

BIRTHDAY WRAP-UP

1. Form 2 teams with players standing side by side.

2. The first player of each team hold a ball of heavy twine.

3. At the signal, he wraps the twine once around his waist, holding end in his hand.

4. He then passes the ball of twine to the next player, who wraps the twine around his waist.

5. Wrapping continues down the line until the last player is wrapped.

6. Then the end player unwraps himself and winds the twine back on the ball.

7. Each player repeats the unwrapping back to first player.

8. When the first player has unwrapped himself and finishes rewinding the ball, the team yells ''Free!''

9. The first team to yell ''Free'' is the winner.

CENTIPEDE RACE

1. Arrange an obstacle course. Use chairs, boxes, small tables, etc. If played outside, trees and bushes can be used as part of the obstacle course.

2. Form 2 teams with players lined up behind each other.

3. Have players of each team crouch in a deep knee bend and place their hands on the hips of player in front. Player at front of line places his hands on his own hips.

4. Team must walk together like a centipede.

5. The object of the game is to go around the obstacle course. The centipede that finishes first is the winner. Give each team a chance to practice first.

BREAK THE BALLOON

1. Give each player a balloon and small rubber band.
2. Have players blow up balloons and tie end with rubber band.
3. Form 2 teams with players lined up behind each other at starting line.
4. Place 2 chairs at far end of room, 1 for each team.
5. At the signal, first player runs to chair with his balloon and sits on balloon until it bursts.
6. He runs back and tags next player in line who does the same.
7. The team that finishes first is the winner.

BALLOON PARTNERS

1. Have players pair off.

2. Give one player of each pair an inflated balloon tied with a string 2' long.

3. Have player tie end of string around one ankle.

4. Then have each pair place their hands around each other's waist. Players must stay "locked" together throughout the game.

5. The object of the game is to stamp on the other players' balloons while keeping his own from breaking.

6. The player with the balloon acts as guard and tries to protect his balloon. His partner acts as stamper and tries to burst opponents' balloons.

7. When a couple's balloon is burst they are eliminated.

8. Game continues until there is only one pair left with their balloon intact. And they are the winners!

Everyone should be exhausted from the last game so here are some quiet games to play before the birthday cake is served.

GUESS WHOSE PICTURE

1. When you send out your invitations on p. 13, ask guests to send a baby photograph of themselves when they reply. As you receive the pictures, have a parent write name on the back to keep a record of who is who. Don't forget to include your own baby picture.

2. Before the party, ask parent to mount the photos with masking tape on a piece of cardboard. Have parent make a list of the names matched to a number, then write the number next to the corresponding photograph. If you let a parent do the paper work, then you won't know the answers and can participate in the game.

3. Give each player pencil and paper. Have players write their names at top of paper.

4. Then have players write the photo numbers in a column down one side of the paper.

5. Tell players to study the pictures and fill in the name next to the number they think corresponds.

6. The winner is the player with the most correct answers.

POP CORN GRAB BOWL

1. Pop enough Jolly Time Pop Corn to fill a large bowl or plastic tub. Use a container you can't see through.

2. Buy an assortment of miniature plastic toys at the dime store.

3. Mix the toys with the pop corn so that they are distributed throughout the entire bowl. Make sure none is showing on top.

4. Give each party guest a paper bag.

5. Tell your guests there are surprises hidden in the pop corn. Then have each guest, in turn, grab a handful. Repeat turns until bowl is empty.

6. Guests get to keep their winnings.

CHRISTMAS

Christmas is a comin' and the geese are getting fat
Please to put a penny in an old man's hat

Not only are the geese getting fat but so are the chickens. Why? Because Jolly Time uses only the center kernels of the cob. These are "choice" kernels that are always tender and always pop crisp. The remainder of the cob is used for chicken feed.

STRINGING POP CORN FOR THE TREE

Decorating the Christmas tree with strings of pop corn is said to date back to the early people of Mexico who used strings of pop corn to decorate idols.

To string pop corn properly, pop it a day or two in advance. If it is too fresh, it breaks easily. Use Jolly Time yellow hulless pop corn, a fine strong needle and a fine but strong thread.

Food coloring can be added if you wish, or put a cranberry between every third or fourth kernel of pop corn on your string for a more colorful look.

PIGTAIL OR PONYTAIL HOLDERS

If you have a friend who wears her hair in a ponytail or braids, this gift makes an attractive replacement for ordinary rubber bands.

1. Raid mother's button box (but first ask her permission) and find 4 matching buttons. Look for the kind that has a shank on the back side. (The holes don't go through the button but sit on the back side only.)
2. Insert a 5'' piece of elastic cord through 2 of the buttons. Tie ends of elastic together in a tight double knot 1/2'' FROM THE ENDS.
3. Move knot close to the button shanks.
4. Give one as a ponytail holder, or make a second one and give the pair as pigtail holders.

JIGSAW PUZZLE—CHRISTMAS GIFT OR CARD

1. Select a photograph or a picture from a magazine or poster. Be sure you choose a picture that the person to whom you are giving it will enjoy.

2. Cut out a piece of thin cardboard a little larger than the size of your picture.

3. Coat one side of the cardboard and the wrong side of the picture with rubber cement. Let set for 1 minute. Carefully press the glue side of the picture to the glue side of the cardboard, smoothing out any wrinkles as you glue.

4. Let dry about 1/2 hour.

5. Cut off cardboard around edge of picture.

6. On the cardboard side, draw irregular lines with pencil. Something like this:

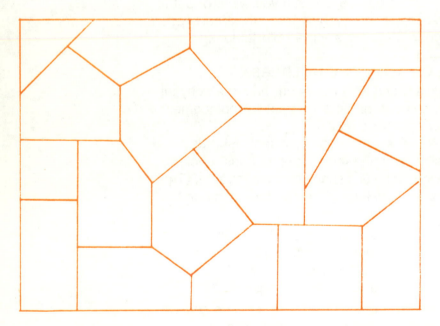

7. Cut the picture into pieces following the lines.

8. Put pieces into a box or envelope and wrap for Christmas.

• *Note:* If you are making the puzzle for a small child, don't cut too many pieces or it will be too difficult to put together.

DECORATIVE BOXES

Have you ever watched your mother search around the house for coupons, maybe in a kitchen drawer full of odds and ends? Or seen your father rummaging through his workshop for nails and screws? Do you have a sister whose hair rollers are scattered all over the place? Or a brother whose desk looks like a tornado hit it?

Well, decorated cigar boxes can solve their problems while making attractive and thoughtful gifts.

Procedure

1. If no one in your family smokes cigars, then go to your neighborhood tobacco store and ask the owner to save the empty boxes for you.

2. Cover them with decorative self-sticking paper which you can buy in dime stores and hardware stores. You can find a pattern to match the color scheme of any room. Or, you can make a collage by cutting up magazine pictures, newspapers, or old photographs and gluing them to the box.

CHRISTMAS TREE PLACE HOLDER

Procedure

1. Make place holder same as invitation on p. 13, following Steps 1 through 4.

2. Print name on one of the branches. Spread sections apart and stand tree up. If tree wobbles, fold flat again and cut off a thin sliver of paper straight across bottom edge.

3. You can cover the inside of the box as well, using a contrasting pattern of self-sticking paper or by gluing on felt or fabric.

4. If you want to designate the box as a special holder, then add a self-adhesive label to the top and print a title such as: STORE COUPONS, HAIR ROLLERS, ODDS AND ENDS. Use your imagination and thoughtfulness to make these special boxes for every member of the family.

POP CORN ORNAMENTS

You will need

Jolly Time Pop Corn—about 1/2 cup stale, un-
  salted popped corn for each ornament
White construction paper or typing paper
Tracing paper
Thin cardboard
Jingle bell for bell ornament (optional)
Sewing needle and white thread
Compass
Scissors
Rubber cement
White craft glue
Pencil

cut ⟶   ⟵ **cut**

Procedure for bell and star

1. Trace star and bell onto 2 separate pieces of
   tracing paper. Cut out shapes.

2. Glue to cardboard with rubber cement. When dry,
   cut out shapes from cardboard to use as patterns.

3. Lay patterns on white paper and trace around the
   edge of patterns with pencil. Cut out. Use patterns again to draw as many bells and stars as
   you like.

Procedure for snowflake

1. With a compass, draw a 5'' diameter circle on
   white paper. Cut out circle.

2. Fold circle in half, fold in half again, then fold in
   half once more.

3. Following broken lines on diagram, cut out wedge
   1/4'' from folded edges. Unfold paper and
   flatten creases.

Decorate cut-outs with pop corn

1. Decorate one ornament at a time. Spread white
   glue evenly on 1 side of cut-out. Wait about 1
   minute allowing glue to dry a little. As glue
   dries it becomes stickier.

2. One by one, press pieces of pop corn onto glue. Place pop corn close together and cover cut-out completely. Break a few loose pieces of pop corn and fill in the small pieces.

3. Let dry thoroughly, about 2 hours.

Hanging loop

With needle and 12" strand of thread, very carefully push needle through paper at top of ornament 1/2" from edge. Tie ends of thread together to make a loop.

Variations: To make an ornament covered with pop corn on both sides, before attaching the hanging loop, glue the paper sides of 2 ornaments together with white glue. If you wish, you can sew a jingle bell to bottom of bell.

HANGING POP CORN BALLS

Use hanging pop corn balls as a door or wall decoration, or hang in an open doorway.

You will need

Jolly Time Pop Corn—about 6 cups popped corn to make 3 balls

Ingredients for making Pop Corn Balls with Molasses Glaze on p. 120 or Pop Corn Balls with Sugar Glaze on p. 118

Green curling ribbon

Red satin ribbon 2'' wide or crepe paper streamer

Scissors

Cellophane tape

Nail or picture hook

Procedure

1. Follow recipe for making pop corn balls and form three 3''-diameter balls. If you use the sugar glaze, you might like to add red or green food coloring. Repeat Steps 2 through 5 for each ball.

2. Cut a 4' piece of curling ribbon and wrap around ball like a package. Secure with knot at top. You'll need an assistant. Have someone hold the ball while you tie.

3. Cut another piece of ribbon 18'' long and tie center of ribbon around knot on ball.

4. Cut a 24'' piece to use as a hanging ribbon. Tie center of ribbon around knot as before.

5. Holding one end of hanging ribbon aside, curl all other ends with edge of scissors.

6. Hold hanging ribbons of all 3 balls together with balls hanging at different levels. Tie ends of hanging ribbons together, then cut off ends 1/2'' from knot. Hang knot on a nail or picture hook.

7. Make a bow with two 4' pieces of satin ribbon or crepe paper held together. Separate the layers of each bow loop. Cut a "V" out of the 4 ends. Attach to hanging knot with cellophane tape.

CHRISTMAS TREE INVITATION

The Christmas tree invitation can also be used as a place holder. See p. 35.

You will need

Green construction paper
Gummed stars
Tracing paper
Thin cardboard
Rubber cement
Stapler
Black felt-tip pen
Pencil
Scissors
Envelopes (3 5/8'' x 6 1/2'')

Procedure

1. Trace tree onto tracing paper. Cut out. Glue to cardboard with rubber cement. When dry, cut out tree from cardboard to use as pattern.

2. Fold edge of construction paper over 2''. Place straight edge of pattern on fold and trace around the edge with pencil. Cut out through double layer of paper. Do not cut paper apart on fold. Unfold tree. Cut out a second tree the same way.

3. Place the 2 trees flat together with bottom edges matching. Staple on fold line placing a staple at top, center, and bottom. Use pattern again and make 2 trees for each invitation required.

4. Glue stars to both sides of all branch tips.

5. Open one section and print CHRISTMAS PARTY. Turn to next section and print TIME information. Turn to next section and print PLACE information. Turn to last section and print R.S.V.P. information. Refer to invitation message on p. 13.

POP CORN CHRISTMAS TREE

You will need

Jolly Time Pop Corn—about 5 quarts popped corn
Ingredients for making Pop Corn Balls with Sugar
  Glaze on p. 118
Styrofoam cone 10'' high
Round toothpicks
Gumdrops or candy kisses wrapped in silver foil

Procedure

1. Following recipe for making pop corn balls, form sixteen 2''-diameter balls and thirty 1 1/2''-diameter balls. Let balls set until firm.

2. Gently push a toothpick half way into each ball.

3. Start at bottom of cone and gently push toothpicks of 8 large balls into cone, spacing balls evenly around.

4. Make a second row with the other 8 large balls. Place each ball between 2 balls of first row. Balls should rest next to balls of last row.

5. Continue making rows using the small balls. Place 1 ball at top.

6. Press toothpicks into flat end of candy kisses or gumdrops. Press into cone through spaces between the balls.

Variations: Balls may be all white, or all one color. Or make a multi-colored tree by dividing pop corn and syrup into separate pots and making each batch a different color.

POP CORN SANTA

You will need

Jolly Time Pop Corn—about 1 cup stale, unsalted
   pop corn for each Santa
Construction paper—red, pink, white, and black
Large red gumdrop for nose
Tracing paper
Thin cardboard
White craft glue
Rubber cement
Masking tape
Compass
Pencil
Scissors

Procedure

1. *Face:* Using compass, draw a 6''-diameter circle
   on pink paper. Cut out.

2. *Cheeks:* Draw two 1-1/2''-diameter circles on
   red paper. Cut out.

3. *Pompom:* Draw one 2''-diameter circle on white
   paper. Cut out.

4. *Eyes:* Cut two 1/2''-diameter circles from black
   paper.

5. Trace hat onto tracing paper. Cut out. Glue to
   cardboard with rubber cement. When dry, cut
   hat from cardboard to use as pattern.

6. Place pattern on red paper and trace around edge
   of pattern with pencil. Cut out. Use pattern
   again to make hats for more Santas.

7. Place hat on top of face circle so that edges of hat
   match edge of circle. Smear glue over area of
   face covered by hat. Press hat in place and
   hold until glue sticks.

8. Glue flat end of gumdrop to center of face. Glue
   on eyes and cheeks as shown. Glue pompom
   to top of hat 1'' from tip.

9. One by one, glue pieces of pop corn: to rim of hat to make a band 1'' wide; to lower half of face for beard; and to pompom. Glue pieces close together. Break a few pieces of loose pop corn to fill in small spaces.

10. Let dry thoroughly, about 2 hours.

11. Cut several 2'' pieces of masking tape. Overlap ends with adhesive side out to make loops.

12. Stick a few loops to back of Santa and carefully press to wall.

13. Make several Santas to decorate the house. Display them on walls, mirrors, doors, and any other place you can think of.

POP CORN SNOWMAN

You will need

Jolly Time Pop Corn—about 6 cups popped corn
Ingredients for making Pop Corn Balls with Sugar Glaze on p. 118
Black licorice stick (cut into small pieces) or chocolate chips for features
Round, glass fish bowl about 4'' diameter for body (optional)
Red crepe paper
Black construction paper
Glitter (optional)
White craft glue
Cellophane tape
Toothpick
Compass
Scissors
Pencil

• *Note:* Snowman's body can be made of a popcorn ball, or fish bowl filled with loose, unsalted popcorn.

Procedure

1. Follow recipe for making pop corn balls using un-colored syrup. Form one 3''-diameter ball for head and one 5''-diameter ball for body. While balls are still sticky, flatten end of body to make base, then press head onto body. Let set until firm. If bowl is used for body, make only the head. Fill bowl to rim with loose, unsalted pop corn. While head is sticky, set on mouth of bowl.

2. *Hat Brim:* Use black construction paper for all parts of hat. Draw a 3'' diameter circle. Then draw a 2'' diameter circle at center of first circle. Cut out large circle, then cut out smaller circle at center to make a donut.

3. *Hat Crown:* Draw a rectangle 6 1/2'' long x 2 1/4'' wide. Cut out. Overlap short ends 1/2'' and tape together on inside of ring. With scissors make cuts 1/4'' deep and 1/4'' apart around each edge of ring.

Bend one clipped edge toward inside of ring for top. Bend other clipped edge toward outside of ring for bottom. Place bottom of ring flat on table. Using toothpick, dab glue on each clipped section. Slide donut over ring to bottom and press against clipped sections. Hold a few seconds until glue sticks.

4. *Hat Top:* Draw a 2'' diameter circle and cut out. Dab glue on each clipped section at top of ring. Gently press circle on top of ring. Hold a few seconds until glue sticks.

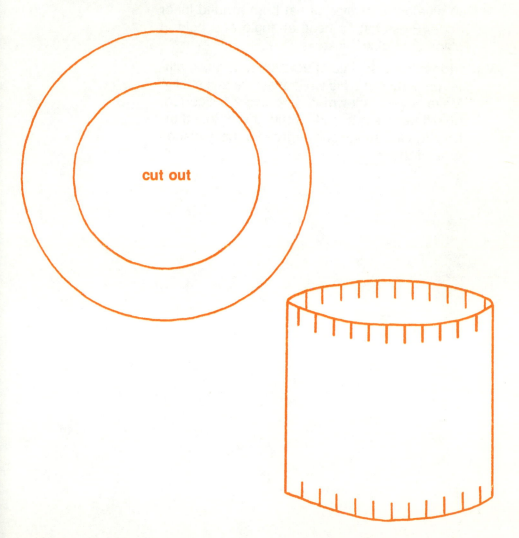

cut out

5. *Scarf:* Cut a rectangle 2'' wide x 15'' long from crepe paper. With scissors, make cuts 1'' deep and 1/8'' apart on short ends for fringe. Fold scarf in half lengthwise and tie around snow-man's neck. Or, use 2'' wide x 15'' long paper ribbon, which can be purchased in winter plaid colors, solids, polka dots, etc.

6. *Features:* Cut licorice stick into small pieces and glue to head to make face. Glue 3 pieces in a row on front of body for buttons. Or, use choc-olate chips instead of licorice.

7. Dab glue on underside of hat brim around inner edge. Press hat on head at angle and hold in place until glue sticks.

Variations: For a sparkle effect, lightly sprinkle glit-ter on pop corn balls while they are still sticky. Make several snowmen, and snow ladies too, of different sizes and group them together. Display with sprigs of evergreen or holly placed around them.

JOLLY TIME DUTCH SHOE

In Holland children expect St. Nicholas to fill their shoes, so we will start with a shoe game.

1. Pop a generous supply of Jolly Time Pop Corn.

2. Form 2 teams with players lined up behind each other at a starting line.

3. Place a bowl of pop corn in front of each team.

4. Place 2 shoes at the other end of the room, 1 for each team.

5. Give starting player of each team a soup spoon.

6. The object of the game is to see which team can fill its shoe with the most pop corn.

7. At the signal, the first player scoops up as much pop corn as he can get on his spoon, then runs to the shoe and pours it in. He runs back and hands the spoon to the next player who repeats the same thing. You cannot use your hands, only the spoon.

8. After players on each team have all had one turn, the team which has filled its shoe with the most pop corn is the winner.

9. Speed counts only in the case of a tie.

THIRTY-ONE

This card game can be played with guests or by the younger members of the family to amuse themselves during the Christmas vacation. It is a variation of blackjack or 21 and is useful for teaching young people to count.

Number of players: 2 to 10

1. Shuffle a deck of cards and deal 3 cards to each player. Players hold the 3 cards in their hands.

2. Place deck face down at center of table.

3. Turn top card face up next to deck. This is the start of the discard pile.

4. The object of the game is to make the total points of your cards add up to 31 points, or as close to 31 as possible.

5. Value of cards: Aces count 11 points each; face cards count 10 points each; all other cards count their face value. For example, if you are holding an ace, a queen, and a 9, you would have 30 points.

6. The player to the left of the dealer starts. He may: a) Keep all of his cards; or b) Draw a card from either the top of the deck or from the top of the discard pile, then discard a card to the pile.

7. Players go in turn. Each player should have 3 cards in his hand after each turn.

8. At any time during the game, a player may "knock" by rapping his hand on the table. When to knock: a) If you are dealt 31 points, knock immediately; b) if the card you draw gives you 31 points, you must wait until your next turn, then knock: c) if the card you draw gives you close to 31 points and you think your hand is higher than the other players, again you must wait until your next turn, then knock.

9. A player takes his turn by *either* drawing a card or knocking, but not both.

10. When a player knocks, the remaining players can each take one more turn to improve their cards. But remember, the player who has knocked cannot draw another card.

Scoring

1. If you are dealt 31, you knock immediately and are given the score of 31 points.

2. If you knock in turn and are holding 31 points, you are given 31 points.

3. If you knock with less than 31 points and your hand is the highest at the table, you are given the value of your hand.

4. If you knock, let's say, with 21 points but another player has a higher hand, the other player gets the total points in his hand and you get a score of minus 10 points.

5. At any time, if a player knocks and his card value is the same as that of another player, then the hand with the highest ranking cards is the winner. For example: first player's hand: ace, queen, and 10 = 31 points; second player's hand: ace, king, and 10 = 31 points. The second hand is higher because the king outranks the queen.

6. The player who reaches 100 points first is the winner.

BLOW THE BALLOON

1. Blow up 1 red balloon and 1 green balloon.

2. Form 2 teams, a red team and a green team.

3. Put the red team on one side of a table and the green team on the other side.

4. Place balloons at center of table.

5. The object of the game is for 1 team to blow the other team's balloon off the table while keeping its own balloon on the table.

6. Everyone must play with his hands behind his back.

7. Players can move around the table after the game starts.

8. A point is scored each time a team blows the opponent's balloon off the table.

9. The first team to score 10 points is the winner.

JOLLY TIME MUSICAL CHAIRS

Musical chairs has been played by children just as long as children have been playing games. But in each country it is called by a different name. In Scotland, for instance, it is called, "Change Seats, The King Is Coming." According to history, this game made fun of politicians scrambling for positions in government when there was a change of kings.

Instead of using the radio or record player, if you have a piano or guitar, play the song.

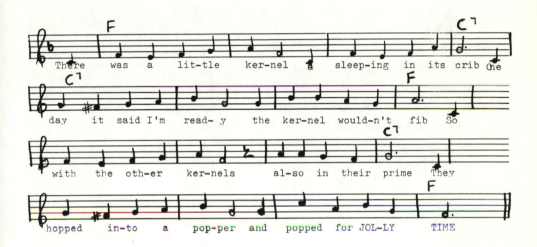

There was a lit-tle ker-nel a sleep-ing in its crib One day it said I'm read-y the ker-nel would-n't fib So with the oth-er ker-nels al-so in their prime They hopped in-to a pop-per and popped for JOL-LY TIME

THE CHRISTMAS TREE FELL DOWN

Did you know that Christmas trees originated in Germany? Trees were already a tradition in the Middle Ages, 500 A.D. to 1400 A.D.

1. All players sit in a circle except one, who stands in the middle of the circle.

2. Each player, including the one in the middle, is given the name of a Christmas tree ornament, such as tinsel, wreath, angel, pop corn string, bell, Santa Claus, star, candy cane.

3. The player in the middle calls out any two ornaments.

4. The players whose names are called must exchange seats.

5. As the two players exchange seats, the middle player tries to get one of the seats.

6. The player left out then goes to the middle.

7. But, at any time, the player in the middle can call out, "The Christmas tree fell down" and then all of the players must change seats.

8. The middle player tries to grab a seat and again the one left standing becomes the middle player.

WHO LIVES IN THE HOUSE?

This game should be prepared before the guests arrive.

1. On separate pieces of paper, draw the house shown below. Draw one house for each guest.

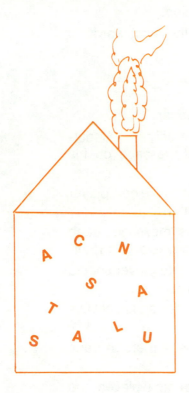

2. Give each player a pencil and a house. Have players write their names at top of paper.

3. Tell players that the person who lives in the house has a first and last name with 5 letters in each name. Also tell them the person is well known to everyone. These are the only clues.

4. The player who unscrambles the letters and discovers the name first is the winner.

5. Set a time limit. Answer on p. 142.

ION GAME

1. Each player gets paper and pencil. Have players write their names at top of paper.
2. The object of the game is to write as many words as you can that end with ION, for example: vacation, action, motion, lotion.
3. The winner is the player with the most words.
4. Set a time limit.

FUNNY CHRISTMAS CARDS

1. Give each player pencil and paper.
2. Have each player write one line only of a Christmas verse or greeting card message on his paper.
3. Each player then folds his paper so the next player cannot see what he has written.
4. After everyone has written his message, each player passes his paper to player on his right.
5. This player writes the next line. No player should repeat a line he has already written.
6. The paper is folded over and passed again, always to the right.
7. Continue until each player has written on each paper.
8. When the papers return to the original players, he or she reads his Christmas card aloud. And gets to keep it!
9. Your funny Christmas card can be attached to one of the gifts you can make on pp. 33, 34 and 35.

EASTER

At Easter let your clothes be new
A gown, a purse, a bonnet will do.
Color your eggs and hide them well
A good Easter bunny will never tell.

The Jolly Time people hide their corn in storage cribs. This gives the corn time to go through a curing process or a rest. Just as you open your windows at night to breathe better with proper ventilation, C.H. Smith built the first crib in 1914 when he discovered that corn popped better after a "rest" than corn taken right from the field.

EASTER EGG INVITATION

You will need

Construction paper—light colors
Tracing paper
Thin cardboard
Crayons or colored pencils
Rubber cement
Black felt-tip pen
Pencil
Scissors
Envelopes (3 5/8'' x 6 1/2'')

place on fold

Procedure

1. Trace egg onto tracing paper. Cut out. Glue to cardboard with rubber cement. When dry, cut egg from cardboard to use as pattern.

2. Fold construction paper in half. Place straight edge of pattern on fold and trace around the edge of pattern with pencil. Cut through double layer of paper. Do not cut apart paper at fold. Use pattern again and make an egg cut-out for each invitation required.

3. Using crayons or colored pencils, decorate the front of egg any way you wish. Color in stripes, flowers, bunnies, or anything else you might think of.

4. On inside, print EASTER PARTY. Refer to invitation message on p. 13 and fill in party information.

TABLECLOTH DECORATION

You will need

Paper tablecloth—solid color
Construction paper—light colors
Tracing paper
Thin cardboard
Rubber cement
White craft glue
Pencil
Crayons or colored pencils
Scissors

Procedure

1. Trace egg on p. 61 onto tracing paper. Cut out. Glue to cardboard with rubber cement. When dry, cut egg from cardboard to use as pattern.

2. Place pattern on construction paper and trace around the edge with pencil. Use pattern again to make as many egg cut-outs as you like.

3. Decorate one side of each egg with crayons or colored pencils. Draw stripes, flowers, bunnies or anything else that would make a nice Easter design.

4. Glue eggs in a scattered arrangement to skirt of tablecloth.

BUNNY CENTERPIECE

You will need

Jolly Time Pop Corn—about 6 cups
Ingredients for making Pop Corn Balls with Sugar
　Glaze on p. 118
Jelly beans—black for eyes, pink for nose
Construction paper—pink, white and yellow
Pipe cleaners—3 pink and 1 white
Round toothpicks
White craft glue
Rubber cement
Scissors
Pencil
Crayons or colored pencils
Thin cardboard
Tracing paper

Procedure

1. Follow recipe for making pop corn balls using un-colored syrup. Form one 3''-diameter ball for head, one 5''-diameter ball for body, and one 1''-diameter ball for tail. While balls are still sticky, flatten ends of body to make base, then press head and tail onto body. Let set until firm. While bunny is drying, make body parts.

2. *Egg:* Trace egg onto tracing paper. Cut out. Glue to cardboard with rubber cement. When dry, cut egg from cardboard to use as pattern. Lay the pattern on yellow construction paper and trace around the edge with pencil. Cut out. Decorate egg with crayons or colored pencils.

3. Make cardboard patterns for foot, hand, and both parts of ear. Cut out 2 pink feet, 2 pink hands, 2 pink inner ears, and 2 white outer ears.

4. *Make Hands:* Cut two 2-1/2'' pieces of pink pipe cleaner. Glue one piece to center of each hand with end extending 1'' beyond straight edge.

5. *Make Ears:* Glue pink inner ears to white outer ears matching straight edges at bottom. Cut two 3-1/2'' pieces of white pipe cleaner. Glue one piece to white side of each ear with end extending 1'' beyond straight edge.

6. *Face:* Nose and Eyes—Break off 1'' end of toothpick. Push point 1/2'' into center front of head. Cut a pink jelly bean in half with knife. Press flat end of half jelly bean over toothpick to make nose. Break 2 more 1'' toothpick ends and push in place for eyes. To make eyes, cut a black jelly bean in half and press half jelly bean in place over toothpicks. Whiskers—Cut two 4'' pieces of pink pipe cleaner. Bend each piece in half. Bend folded end up 1/2'' as shown. Press 1/2'' end of each whisker into head below nose.

outer
ear

inner
ear

7. *Assemble Body Parts:* Feet—Smear glue 1/2"
   wide across straight edge of each foot. Press
   to bottom of body. Hold in place a few seconds
   until glue sticks. Ears—Press end of pipe
   cleaner into top of head. Pink sides of ears face
   toward front. Hand and Egg—Press end of pipe
   cleaner into each side of body with pipe cleaner
   facing toward front. Gently curve hand toward
   front. Place a dab of white glue at tip of hand
   on same side as pipe cleaner. Press tips of
   hands over edges of egg. Hold in place a few
   seconds until glue sticks.

8. Set bunny on a bed of Easter grass at center of
   party table. Sprinkle jelly beans over the grass.

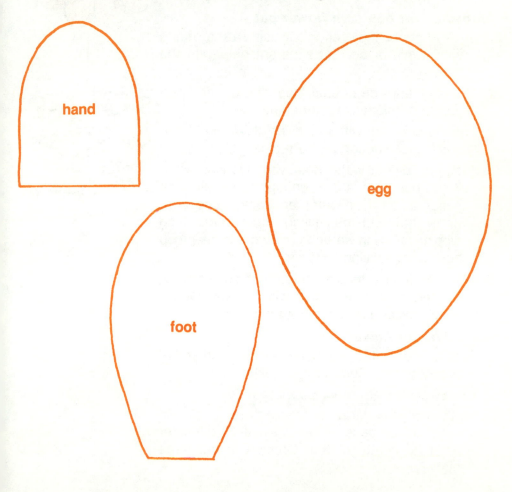

FLOWER POT PLACE HOLDER

You will need

Jolly Time Pop Corn—about 1 cup for each place holder

Ingredients for making Pop Corn Balls with Molasses Glaze on p. 120, or Pop Corn Balls with Sugar Glaze on p. 118

Flat, round lollipops with cellophane wrappers

Construction paper—assorted colors

Styrofoam beverage cups—1 cup for each place holder

Awl or nail

Compass

White craft glue

Procedure for pop corn flower pot

1. Slice 1'' off the top of each cup using a sharp knife with a thin blade. Let a parent help with the cutting.

2. Grease the inside of each cup with butter, margarine or vegetable shortening.

3. Prepare pop corn with molasses glaze or colored sugar glaze according to recipe.

4. Place a bowl of water near your working area. When pop corn is cool enough to handle, wet hands in bowl of water and press pop corn firmly into each cup filling cup to rim. Keep dipping hands in water as you work to keep pop corn from sticking to them.

5. Wait 10 minutes, then unmold. Push pop corn out by pressing bottom of cup with thumbs. Gently ease molded pop corn from cup.

Procedure for flower

1. Press awl or nail 1'' into center of the wide end of pop corn pot. Remove.

2. Gently push stem of lollipop into hole.

3. With compass, draw a 3''-diameter circle on construction paper. Then draw a 1''-diameter circle at center of first circle. Cut out large circle.

4. *Petals:* Cut from edge toward inner circle as shown by broken lines in diagram. Cuts should be about 1/2'' apart at outer edge.

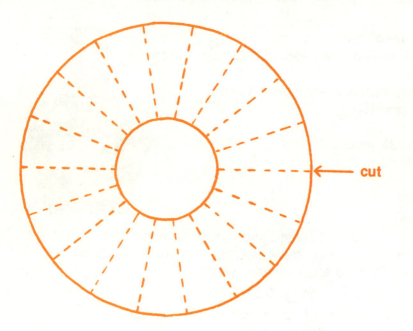

cut

5. Cut end of each petal in a curve. Bend petals toward unmarked side.

6. Print name at center. Glue back of flower to lollipop wrapper.

EASTER BASKET FAVOR

Baskets are taped together, not stapled, to eliminate the danger of staples falling into food. Basket can also be used as a place holder by attaching a name tag.

You will need

Jolly Time Pop Corn—about 1/2 cup for each basket
Construction paper—assorted colors
Easter grass
Ruler
White craft glue
Cellophane tape
Pencil
Scissors

Procedure

1. Cut a 6'' square from construction paper for each basket. Using ruler, mark each 6'' square as shown. Be sure all sides are even.

2. Cut on the solid lines and fold on the broken lines.

3. *Forming Basket:* Hold up section marked A as side of basket. Bring corners marked B together on outside of A to make a point. Hold all 3 sections together and tape along top edge of A on inside. Then tape outside sections together. Make other side the same.

4. *Handle:* Cut a 3/4'' x 6'' strip from construction paper for each basket. Tape ends to points on inside.

5. Cut a small square from a piece of construction paper a different color from basket for name tag. Print name on tag and glue to side of basket.

6. Line basket with Easter grass and fill with pop corn and jelly beans.

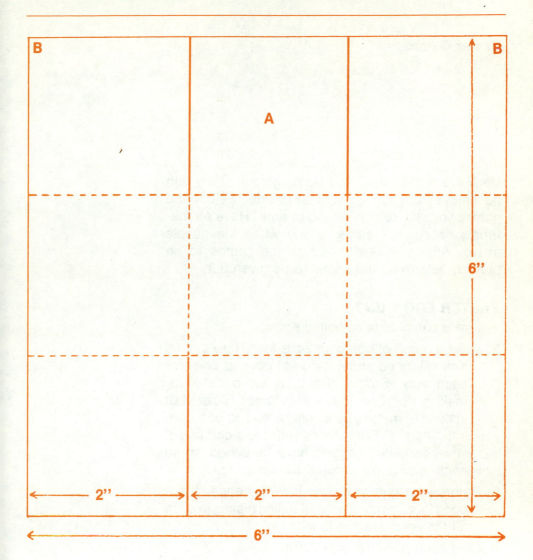

B A B

6"

2" 2" 2"

6"

Easter Games

Here are some rabbit and bunny games. They can be enjoyed outside as well as inside. Select the games you plan to play ahead of time. Have all materials needed for games ready when the guests arrive. After you've decided on the games to be played, determine the prizes to be given out.

EASTER EGG HUNT

1. Dye a batch of hard-boiled eggs.
2. Make a batch of pop corn eggs too! Here's how. You will need about 1 cup of popped corn for each egg. Follow directions on p. 118 for making Pop Corn Balls with Sugar Glaze, but instead of making balls, shape glazed pop corn into "eggs." Color them with food coloring if you like. After "eggs" have hardened, wrap each in silver or colored aluminum foil.
3. Before your guests arrive, hide the eggs. It's a good idea to make a list of hiding places in case all the eggs are not found.
4. Give each player a paper bag.
5. The object of the game is for each player to find as many eggs as he can.
6. Set a time limit.
7. Scoring: Each hard-boiled egg counts 2 points; each pop corn egg counts 4 points.
8. The player with the highest score is the winner.

BUNNY HOP BALLOON RACE

1. Give each player a balloon and a small rubber band.

2. Have each player blow up his own balloon and tie end with rubber band.

3. Place a large box about 20' from starting line.

4. Put all balloons in the box. Blow up a few extra balloons and place in box.

5. Form two teams with players lined up behind each other at starting line.

6. At the signal, first player on each team runs to box, gets a balloon and puts it between his legs.

7. Player must hop back to next player in line keeping balloon between his legs.

8. If balloon falls, player must put it back between his legs and continue hopping. If balloon bursts, player must go back to box, get another balloon, and start back from box again.

9. Team to finish first is the winner.

POP CORN PASS

1. Form two teams with players lined up behind each other.

2. Give each player a teaspoon.

3. At the front of each line, place a bowl containing the same number of pop corn pieces as there are players in the line. (If there are six players on each team, there should be six pieces of pop corn in each bowl.)

4. Place an empty bowl at the end of each line.

5. The object of the game is to empty the first bowl and fill the second one.

6. At the signal, the first player scoops up one piece of pop corn onto his spoon. He then transfers the piece of pop corn onto the spoon of the player who does the same thing with the next player.

7. The last player in line drops the pop corn from his spoon into the empty bowl and runs to the front of the line. The pop corn pass is repeated until all players have had their turn at the front of the line.

8. When the original first player drops the last piece of pop corn into the bowl and runs back to the front of the line, he yells "Pop corn!"

9. The first team to yell "Pop corn!" is the winner.

10. If a piece of pop corn falls off a spoon during play, the player must scoop it back on and continue playing. (He can use his fingers to push it onto the spoon, but he cannot pick it up.)

THE MILL WHEEL

Here is a song for the guests to learn before the start of an old-fashioned Scots game known as The Mill Wheel. It is always fun to make your own music as the tune just falls into place.

There was a jolly miller   One hand on the hopper
And he lived by himself   And another in the bag
As the wheel went round   As the wheel went round
He made his wealth   He made his grab

1. Each boy chooses a girl partner.

2. Form a large ring with the boys inside and the girls outside.

3. The left over boy is the Miller. If a girl is left over, she can be the Miller and can hold a handkerchief to show she is the Miller.

4. The Miller stands inside the ring and as the wheel turns, boys go in one direction, girls in another, they start to sing the song.

5. At the word "grab" all boys move forward one place while the Miller tries to secure a partner.

6. If the Miller succeeds then the leftover boy is the new Miller.

7. If not, then the wheel begins again and the song is sung and the same boy starts in the center as the Miller.

There are many variations to this game but it is the jingle from a faraway country that makes this variation a charming one.

PIN THE TAIL ON THE BUNNY

This is a variation on the donkey game, but more fun because you have made the game yourself.

BUNNY TAILS

You will need

Ingredients for making the Pop Corn Balls with Sugar Glaze on p. 118

White paper

White craft glue

Black felt-tip pen

Mounting tape (This tape is usually found with the picture-hanging accessories in dime stores. It has an adhesive surface on both sides separated by a foam cushion.)

Procedure

1. Follow directions for making pop corn balls. Tails can be colored with food coloring if you like. Two tails are made from one ball. Make enough balls so that each party guest will have a tail.

2. After balls have hardened, cut each in half with a sharp kitchen knife. Let a parent help with the cutting.

3. Cut 1'' pieces of mounting tape and stick a piece to the flat side of each tail. Do not remove protective covering on front side of tape until you are ready to play the game.

4. Cut a 3/4''-diameter circle from white paper for each tail. Starting with the number 1, write a different number on each circle with black pen. Glue a number to front of each tail.

5. Because of tape and glue, tails should not be eaten after the game.

BUNNY DRAWING

You will need

White paper 18'' wide x 36'' long. (Art stores sell large sheets of drawing paper.) If you can't get

a piece large enough, glue two pieces together.

Compass
Pencil
Black crayon

Procedure

1. With compass, draw three circles on the large
   sheet of paper as shown in diagram. Draw ears.

2. Trace over lines with black crayon. Draw broken
   lines on tail circle.

Playing the game

1. Tape your Easter Bunny with masking tape to a
   wall with lots of space.

2. Mark a starting line about 12' from bunny drawing.

3. Give each player a pop corn bunny tail. Tell
   players to remember their numbers. Have them
   remove the protective paper on front of the
   tape.

4. Blindfold each player in turn, spin him around
   three times, and start him off in direction of
   bunny.

5. The object of the game is to see which player
   comes closest to placing his tail in the circle
   where the tail belongs.

8"

12"

3"

HOP LIKE A RABBIT

1. Form two teams with players lined up behind each other at starting line.

2. Using two chairs, place a chair about 12' in front of each team.

3. Squat with knees spread apart and place hands on floor between knees. Move hands forward and bring feet up to hands with a jump!

4. The object of the game is to hop to chair, go around it, and come back to the starting line. Then the next player takes his turn.

5. The team that finishes first is the winner. It might be a good idea to let everyone practice hopping before beginning the game.

TEST YOUR MEMORY

1. Set up a card table.

2. Place on the table 15 different items that can be easily identified. Choose objects such as a book, toy plane, spoon, bar of soap, kitchen plate, scissors, etc. Leave spaces between items.

3. Cover the objects with a tablecloth.

4. Give each player pencil and paper. Have players write their names at top of paper.

5. Whip off the cloth for a count of five, then re-cover the objects.

6. Have players list as many items as they can remember.

7. Set a time limit.

"E" GAME

1. Give each player pencil and paper. Have players write their names at top of paper.

2. The object of the game is to write as many words as they can think of that begin with the letter E.

3. The player who writes the most words is the winner.

4. Set a time limit.

HALLOWEEN

Hey-how for Halloween
The witches can be seen
Riding alone on a funny broom
Did they sweep away their groom?

And if they did indeed sweep away their groom then they were old maid witches! Did you know that there are corn kernels called "old maids"? These are the kernels that do not pop open. But how do we know which corn will pop? Because the corn that pops is very different from other corn in starchy content. The American Indians cultivated as many as 700 varieties of corn but only one variety popped open when exposed to heat. They believed the corn that popped in the sun or heat had a demon inside of it. The maker of Jolly Time learned which type of corn pops open, they began to grow it, and now produce and package it—corn that will not pop on the ear but pops in the pan and then is popped into your mouth.

POP CORN BOWL CENTERPIECE

You will need

Jolly Time Pop Corn—about 4 quarts popped
corn to make bowl and about 2 quarts loose,
salted pop corn to fill bowl

Ingredients for making Pop Corn Balls with Sugar
Glaze on p. 118

Red and yellow food coloring

Mixing bowl about 6'' high x 10'' top diameter

Aluminum foil

Waxed paper

1 yard black ribbon

Procedure

1. Line bowl with aluminum foil so that ends of foil
   hang over rim of bowl. Lightly grease foil with
   oil or vegetable shortening.

2. Follow recipe for making pop corn balls. Color
   syrup orange by adding equal amounts of red
   and yellow coloring. Mix syrup with pop corn.

3. When pop corn is cool enough to handle, pack
   tightly into bowl covering entire inner surface.
   Pack pop corn 1'' thick all around.

4. Let set about 10 minutes, then unmold. Pull on
   edges of foil to lift pop corn from mixing bowl.

5. Place pop corn bowl upside down on waxed paper
   and carefully remove foil.

6. Tie the black ribbon around pop corn bowl 1½''
   from rim to strengthen sides.

7. Let stand upside down overnight, then fill with
   loose, salted pop corn.

NAPKIN RING

You will need

 Black licorice whips
 Lollipops
 Paper napkins

Procedure

1. Cut licorice whips into 9'' lengths, one piece for each napkin ring.
2. Form a ring with licorice by tying a square knot leaving 2'' ends.
3. Unfold napkin and draw center through licorice ring.
4. Insert lollipop stick through knot.

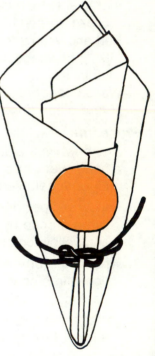

POP CORN BALL ON A STICK

You will need

Jolly Time Pop Corn—about 2 cups popped corn for each ball

Ingredients for Pop Corn Balls with Molasses Glaze on p. 120

Salted peanuts (optional)—about 1 tablespoon for each ball

Wood ice cream sticks, or thin wood dowels cut 5½'' long

Colored cellophane paper or clear plastic wrap

Curling ribbon

Scissors

Procedure

1. Make pop corn balls following recipe. If you like, peanuts can be mixed in with the glazed pop corn.

2. While balls are still soft, push a wood stick into each.

3. Cut a 13'' square from cellophane or plastic wrap for each ball. Cut three 15'' pieces of curling ribbon for each ball.

4. After balls have hardened, wrap cellophane around each ball gathering ends up around stick. Holding the three ribbons together, tie center of ribbons in a double knot around gathered paper. Curl ribbons with edge of scissors.

POP CORN CANDY CORN FAVOR

1. Follow recipe on p. 118 for making Pop Corn Balls with Sugar Glaze. You will need about 3 cups popped corn for each candy corn.

2. When syrup is ready, pour a quarter of it into a second pot, and another quarter into a third pot. Keep the remaining half in the original, first pot. Add equal amounts of red and yellow food coloring (to make orange) to the first pot containing half of the syrup. Add yellow only to the second pot. Leave third pot clear.

3. Place the hot pop corn in 3 separate bowls, dividing it in the same proportion as the syrup. Pour yellow syrup over a quarter of the pop corn, clear syrup over the other quarter and orange syrup over the remaining half. Mix syrup thoroughly.

4. Following diagram, shape pop corn into triangles each about 1'' thick. Serve on paper plate.

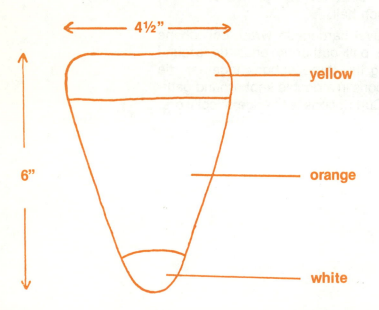

TRICK OR TREAT GOODIES

You will need

Jolly Time Pop Corn—about 2 cups salted, popped corn for each bag

Candy corn—about ¼ cup for each bag

Plastic sandwich bags

Curling ribbon

Procedure

1. Fill each bag with pop corn and candy corn.

2. Cut three 14'' pieces of curling ribbon.

3. Holding the three pieces of ribbon together, gather up top edge of bag and tie center of ribbons around bag in a double knot.

4. Curl ends of ribbon with edge of scissors.

JACK O'LANTERN SANDWICHES

1. Cut two pieces of bread into large circles. Cut eyes, nose and mouth out of one piece.

2. Spread bottom piece with peanut butter, ham salad, cold cuts or whatever other spreads you prefer.

3. Place cut out slice of bread on top and fill in features with pop corn.

PUMPKIN PLACE HOLDER

The pumpkins are edible. Have guests take their place holders home.

You will need

> Jolly Time Pop Corn—about 2 cups popped corn for each pumpkin
> Ingredients for making Pop Corn Balls with Sugar Glaze on p. 118
> Red and yellow food coloring
> Black construction paper
> White construction paper or typing paper
> Orange pipe cleaners
> Tracing paper
> Thin cardboard
> White craft glue
> Rubber cement
> Black felt-tip pen
> Pencil
> Scissors

Procedure

1. Following recipe for making pop corn balls, form 3″-diameter balls using orange syrup. Add equal amounts of red and yellow food coloring to make orange. As you form each ball, flatten one side for base. Make one ball for each place holder. Let pumpkins set until firm.

2. Trace cat onto tracing paper. Cut out. Glue to cardboard with rubber cement. When dry, cut cat from cardboard to use as pattern.

3. Place pattern on black paper and trace around the edge of pattern with pencil. Cut out. Use pattern again to make a cat cut-out for each pumpkin.

4. Cut eyes from white paper and glue cat's face as shown.

5. Cut a small rectangle from white paper and print name at center with black pen. Glue to cat's body.

6. Cut pipe cleaner into 4½'' pieces. Glue length-wise to back of cat with pipe cleaner extending 1'' below feet. Push into top of pumpkin after pumpkins have hardened. (It may be necessary to first make a hole in top of pumpkin using an awl or nail before inserting pipe cleaner.)

GHOST INVITATION

You will need

White construction paper or typing paper
Tracing paper
Thin cardboard
Rubber cement
Black felt-tip pen
Pencil
Scissors
Envelopes (3 5/8" x 6 1/2")

Procedure

1. Trace ghost onto tracing paper. Cut out. Glue to cardboard with rubber cement. When dry, cut ghost from cardboard to use as pattern.

2. Fold white paper in half. Place straight edge of pattern on fold and trace around the edge of pattern with pencil. Cut out through double layer of paper. Do not cut paper apart on fold. Use pattern again and make a ghost cut-out for each invitation required.

3. Refer to diagram and draw eyes on front using black pen. Print BOO! on front.

4. On inside, print HALLOWEEN PARTY. Refer to invitation message on p. 13 and fill in party information.

place on fold

BOO!

Halloween Games

Look over these games and decide ahead of time which ones you'll be playing so you will know how much pop corn to prepare.

POP CORN RELAY

1. Form two teams.
2. Mark a starting line at one end of the room and a goal line at the other end.
3. Give each player a blunt table knife and one piece of pop corn.
4. The object of the game is to walk to the goal line and back while balancing the pop corn on the knife.
5. If pop corn falls off, replace it and continue from the point where it dropped. You do not have to start from the beginning of the line again.
6. The team that finishes first is the winner.

CRAZY WILD CARD

Number of Players: 2 to 6

1. One player draws a card from the deck. This card is the "wild card" and the other three cards of the same face value are also wild cards. For instance, if the 10 of clubs is drawn, all 10s are wild.

2. Replace wild card in deck and shuffle.

3. Deal each player 7 cards if two people are playing. Deal each player 5 cards if more than two people are playing.

4. Place remaining cards face down at center of table. Turn top card up next to deck. This is the start of the discard pile.

5. If the first card turned up is a wild card, bury it in the deck and turn over the next card.

6. Arrange your hand according to suit.

7. Player to left of dealer begins. He selects a card from his hand that matches the card in the discard pile and places it on top of the pile.

8. A matching card is: a) A card of the same suit (heart on a heart, spade on a spade, etc.); b) a card with the same face value (8 on an 8, queen on a queen, etc.); or c) a wild card may be played.

9. If player cannot play, he must draw a card from the deck. He continues to draw until he draws a card he can play.

10. A wild card may be used to change the suit if it's to a player's advantage. Let's say the top card on the discard pile is an 8 of clubs. If 3's are wild, you may play your 3 and name another suit. Good strategy is to call the suit of which you have the most cards.

11. The first player to get rid of all his cards wins the hand, and collects all the points from the other players' hands. The first player to get 500 points wins the game.

12. Scoring: Wild cards count 50 points; face cards count 10 points; aces and all other cards count 5 points.

• *Note:* If all cards have been drawn from the deck and no one can make a play on the discard pile, the winner is the player with the least number of points in his hand and he collects the points in the other players' hands. Or, you can shuffle the discard pile, leaving the last discard down and play continuously until someone goes out.

DOUBLE UP

1. Give each player pencil and paper. Have players write their names at top of paper.

2. The object of the game is to write as many words as you can think of that contain double letters. For instance: ba*ll*, d*ee*p, Ha*ll*ow*ee*n.

3. Scoring: 5 points for each word with one set of double letters; 10 points for each word with two sets of double letters.

4. The winner is the player with the highest score.

5. Set a time limit.

PITCH THE POP CORN IN THE PUMPKIN

1. Place a plastic or real pumpkin on the floor next to a wall. If a real pumpkin is used, line the inside with aluminum foil to keep pop corn from getting soggy.

2. Give each player six pieces of pop corn.

3. Mark a tossing line a few feet from the pumpkin. Let younger children stand closer than older children.

4. The object of the game is to toss the pop corn *underhanded*, one piece at a time, into the top opening of the pumpkin.

5. Select a scorekeeper to keep track of the number of pieces each player tosses into the pumpkin.

6. The player who scores the highest is the winner.

7. The prize could be the pumpkin filled with pop corn!

NINE LIVES OF THE BLACK CATS

1. Make 18 black cats following Steps 2 through 4 of place holders on p. 82.

2. Hide cats before guests arrive.

3. Form two teams.

4. The object of the game is to find the hidden cats.

5. The first team to find nine cats is the winner.

SPOOKY HAND

While your guests are resting from the apple and corn bob, entertain them with this spooky bit of magic.

1. With fingers together, place one hand flat on a table.

2. Slide a playing card under your hand from tips of fingers toward palm.

3. One at a time, slide 4 more cards under your hand.

4. Then say the magic words,
        Hey-how for Halloween
         The ghost in my hand
          Cannot be seen

5. Raise your hand and all the cards will come off the table.

Explanation: Before you do the trick, put a toothpick under the ring you are wearing! Place the toothpick on the palm side of your hand so it is parallel to your finger. Slide the first card under your hand between your fingers and the toothpick. Slide the other 4 cards under your hand on top of the first card. When you lift your hand the toothpick will hold the cards. Be sure to keep your palm facing down so you don't expose the toothpick.

GEORGE THE GHOST

Before your guests arrive, write a short message on a blank piece of white paper using a toothpick or thin brush dipped in lemon juice. Keep dipping the brush or toothpick in the juice as you write.

At some point during the party, tell your guests you know a friendly ghost named George. In fact, he helped you with the last trick. Look around the room and "discover" the blank piece of paper. "Oh," you say, "there's a message from George!" You pick it up and "read" it and begin to laugh. Then tell your friends you will share it with them.

Heat the paper over a toaster and slowly George's words will appear.

CHANGE THE LETTERS

1. Give each player pencil and paper. Have players write their names at top of paper.
2. Tell each player to write these four words across the top of his paper: HOPE, LOVE, BACK, GAME.
3. The object of the game is to substitute just one letter of each word with another letter, forming a new word. Any letter can be changed. For example:

HOPE	LOVE	BACK	GAME
dope	dove	rack	lame
mope	cove	pack	tame
hole	lope	buck	gate
home	lose	bark	gave

4. The winner is the player with the most words.
5. Set a time limit.

POP CORN GUESSING GAME

1. Before the guests arrive, fill a medium size, clear glass jar with pop corn, counting the pieces as you fill it. Close jar with lid.

2. Write the total number on a piece of paper. Put the paper in a safe place so you can refer to it in case you forget the number.

3. Early in the party, bring out the pop corn jar.

4. Give each player pencil and paper. Have players write their names at top of paper.

5. Tell players to guess the number of pieces in the jar. Give them a few minutes to look it over.

6. After players have written their guesses, collect the papers.

7. Keep your guests in suspense (after all, it's Halloween) and announce the winner later.

8. The player whose guess is closest to the actual number is the winner.

VANISHING WATER

And for your final Halloween prank, you and George will make some water disappear.

Fill an ordinary drinking glass half full of water. Tape the bottom of the glass to a table with adhesive or masking tape. Three or four strips should convince your friends that the glass can't be moved. ask someone to turn off the lights. Tell them, "George only works in the dark." Stamp your feet and rap on the table. When the lights are turned back on, the water will be gone.

Explanation: You have a straw in your pocket! After the lights are turned off, quickly slip the straw into the glass and drink the water, but leave a little in the bottom so no sucking noise will be heard. You stamp your feet and rap on the table to cover up any drinking sounds. Don't forget to put the straw back in your pocket before the lights are turned on.

If your friends have never seen this trick, they will be amazed.

POP CORN AND APPLE BOB

1. Prepare a pop corn ball for each guest: Cut a piece of lightweight string 4' long for each pop corn ball. Form a 3''-diameter ball around the end of each string following recipe on p. 120 for Pop Corn Balls with Molasses Glaze, or recipe on p.118 for Pop Corn Balls with Sugar Glaze.

2. Prepare an apple for each guest: Cut a 4' piece of string for each apple and tie one end around stem.

3. Secure the ends of a clothesline about 6' from the floor.

4. Tie apples and pop corn balls to clothesline at varying heights. Balls and apples should be adjusted to same height as each child's mouth.

5. The object of the game is to grab onto an apple or pop corn ball with your teeth, keeping hands held behind your back.

6. The prize is the apple or pop corn ball you have caught.

7. A special prize could be given to the player who captures both an apple and a pop corn ball.

CARD READING

This game is suggested for older children.

1. Tell your guests that you can read cards through your finger tips.

2. Ask a guest to shuffle a deck of cards in full view of everyone.

3. Have him place one card from the deck face down on the palm of your hand.

4. You are standing by a light switch. You explain that in order to receive an impression, you must have total darkness.

5. Switch off the light and say, "I get a mental image of a three . . . Let's see, yes, a three . . . a three of spades."

6. Turn the light switch back on. Turn over the card and lo and behold it is the three of spades.

7. Astound your friends by identifying 6 more cards the same way.

Explanation: Arrange cards before your guests arrive. The ranking of the suits are spades, hearts, diamonds, clubs. Remove 7 cards from a full deck of playing cards in the order of your telephone number as well as in the order of the suits.

For instance: Let's say your phone number is 395-2172. Take out the 3 of spades, 9 of hearts, 5 of diamonds, 2 of clubs, ace of spades, 7 of hearts, 2 of diamonds. Place these cards in this order in your left pocket.

Have a guest shuffle the remaining cards of the deck (no one will notice that 7 cards are missing) and place one card face down on your palm. You switch off the light and switch cards. Slip the card on your palm into your right pocket and pull out the first card from your left pocket and place this one on your palm.

You know the order of the suits and you know your telephone number, so all you have to do is go into your act. Repeat your finger reading technique for all 7 cards. Don't repeat the trick.

THANKSGIVING

Thanksgiving is always a family affair
Sometimes we ask our friends in to share—
The turkey, stuffing, cranberries and such
Have a jolly good time but don't eat too much!

When the Pilgrims created the time of thanks, the American Indians brought their food to share at the dinner: the Indians brought corn, which they called "maize." They used the corn for decorations in their teepees and on their bodies. As far back as 300 A.D. a funeral urn was made in Mexico depicting a maize god with pop corn in his headdress. Until the late 19th century, pop corn remained an at-home treat but with the coming of carnivals, circuses and county fairs, pop corn began to be shared by all kinds of people. Even today we share it at the movies. Let's not forget our Indian friends who taught us to eat and to love pop corn.

POP CORN CANDLE HOLDER

You will need

Jolly Time Pop Corn—about 2 cups popped corn for each holder

Ingredients for making Pop Corn Balls with Sugar Glaze on p. 118 or Pop Corn Balls with Molasses Glaze on p. 120

Candles 8'' tall

• *Note:* Pop corn can be coated with either the sugar glaze used clear or colored with food coloring, or the molasses glaze. Holders can be stored to re-use at Christmas by wrapping in aluminum foil.

Procedure

Follow recipe for making pop corn balls, forming a 3''-diameter ball for each candle holder. As you form each ball flatten one end for base. Use finger to poke 1''-diameter hole 1'' deep at the opposite end molding ball to keep it round. Set aside until holders have hardened.

Suggested uses: Place 2 holders on dining table, one at each side of Indian Corn Centerpiece on p. 102, or group several in a circle. Place fall leaves around them if you like. Display throughout the house on coffee table, end tables or mantelpiece.

Caution: Do not let candles burn too low. Holders may burn.

POP CORN BALL TURKEY

Make a turkey for each dinner guest and set one at each place setting. Turkeys can be eaten after removing paper parts.

You will need

Jolly Time Pop Corn—about 2 1/2 cups popped corn for each turkey
Ingredients for making Pop Corn Balls with Molasses Glaze on p. 120
Orange construction paper
Compass
Pencil
Scissors
White craft glue

Procedure

1. *Tail:* With a compass, draw a 4''-diameter circle on orange paper. Then draw a 1'' circle at center. Cut out 4'' circle. Fold circle in half with small circle on outside. Cut paper from edge to inner circle making cuts 3/8'' apart at outer edges. Dab glue inside center circle and hold halves together until glue sticks.

2. *Wings:* Draw 3''-diameter circle on orange paper, then draw 1''-diameter circle at center. Fold circle in half and crease. Unfold paper and cut on fold line to make 2 semi-circles. Fold semi-circle in half with small circle on outside. Cut paper from edge to inner circle making cuts 1/4'' apart on outer edge. Fold center point over 1/4''. Make second wing the same using the other semi-circle.

3. Following recipe, make a 3''-diameter pop corn ball for body and a 1''-diameter ball for head for each turkey. Flatten one side of large ball for base. While balls are still sticky, press head to body and hold in place until set.

4. Assemble bird while balls are still sticky. Press tail to back of body. Press folded points of wings to sides of body.

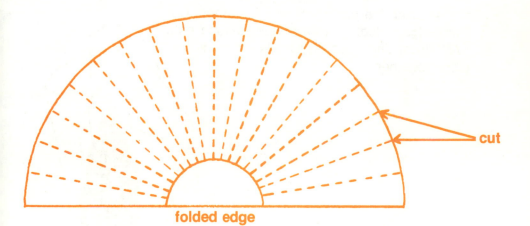

cut

folded edge

FEATHER NAPKIN RING

You will need
Brown and yellow construction paper
Napkin
Tracing paper
Thin cardboard
White craft glue
Rubber cement
Pencil
Ruler
Scissors

Procedure
1. Trace feather onto tracing paper. Cut out. Glue to cardboard with rubber cement. When dry, cut feather from cardboard to use as pattern.

2. Place pattern on brown paper and trace around edge of pattern with pencil. Cut out. Use pattern again to make additional feathers.

3. Draw straight line down center of feather. Cut from edge of feather toward line, ending cuts 1/8'' from line. Cut diagonally making cuts close together.

4. Cut a band 1/2'' wide x 6'' long from yellow paper.

5. Overlap short ends 1/2'' to form a ring and glue ends together. Hold ends a few seconds until glue sticks.

6. Glue center of feather to seam of band.

7. Unfold napkin and draw center of napkin through ring.

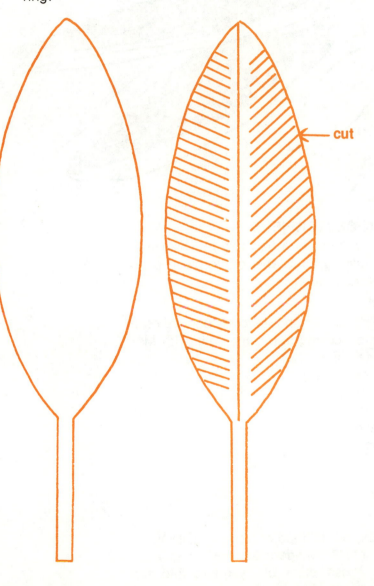

cut

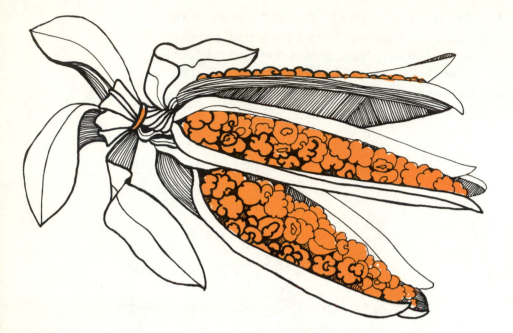

INDIAN CORN CENTERPIECE

Three ears of pop corn are tied together like real Indian corn to display as a table centerpiece or to hang as a wall decoration.

You will need

Jolly Time Pop Corn—about 9 cups popped corn
Ingredients for making Pop Corn Balls with Molasses Glaze on p. 120
Thin brown paper bags
String—one piece cut 12'' long
Cellophane tape
3 rubber bands
Straight pins
Ruler.
Pencil
Scissors

Procedure

1. Follow recipe, but instead of making balls, form pop corn into 3 cylinders each 8'' long x 2'' diameter. Press ends of cylinders into the shape of an ear of corn.

2. From brown paper bags cut 14 rectangles each 3'' wide x 14'' long.

3. Cut one end of each rectangle into a rounded point to make a leaf.

4. Place 3 leaves together as shown.

5. Tape leaves where they overlap 7'' from straight edge. Turn leaves over and tape overlap at center 7'' from straight edge. The 3 leaves together form the husk.

6. While corn is still sticky, place one ear lengthwise at center of husk 2'' from points. Wrap edges of husk around ear. Gather up straight edge of husk and twist tightly to form a stem. Be sure to twist paper hard enough to keep it from untwisting.

7. Stretch a rubber band around corn 2'' from stem to hold husk. Push a few straight pins through husk into ears near stem.

8. Make 2 other ears the same way.

9. Hold the 3 ears together by their stems. Hold the 5 other leaves together with straight ends at top. Place the leaves behind the stems and gather together. Tie center of string tightly around gathered paper and knot securely.

10. Tie ends of string together to make a hanging loop.

11. Leave the 2 outer leaves in place. Pull up the other 3 leaves so they stand up around stems. Fold each of the 3 leaves in half lengthwise and crease. Unfold and tightly roll up each leaf. Let leaves unroll themselves. Remove rubber bands.

Caution: Because of the straight pins used in the assembly, *do not eat corn!*

PILGRIM'S HAT PLACE HOLDER

You will need

Construction paper—gray, black and yellow
Tracing paper
Thin cardboard
Rubber cement
Black felt-tip pen
Pencil
Scissors
Envelopes (3 5/8'' x 6 1/2'')

Procedure

1. Trace hat onto tracing paper. Cut out. Glue to cardboard with rubber cement. When dry, cut hat from cardboard to use as pattern.

2. Place pattern on gray paper and trace around edge of pattern with pencil. Cut out. Use pattern again and make a hat for each invitation required.

3. Make a pattern for band same as hat and cut a band from black paper.

4. *Buckle:* Cut a 1'' square from yellow paper. Cut out center of square as shown.

5. Glue band to hat just above rim. Glue buckle to center of band.

6. Print name on crown of hat using black pen.

7. Cut a piece of thin cardboard 1/2'' wide x 3'' long. Fold over one end 1/2''. Glue short folded end to center back of hat for stand.

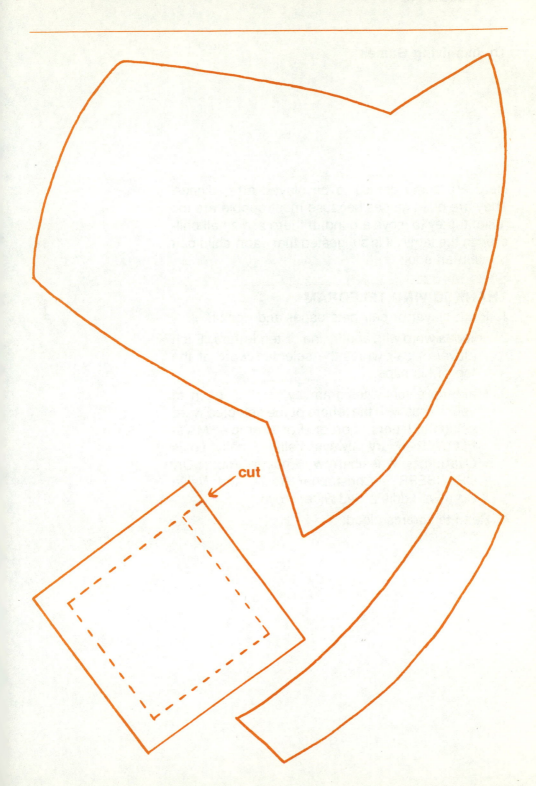

cut

Thanksgiving Games

Here are some games to be played after dinner. They are quiet games because most people are too full of turkey to move around. If there are small children in the family it is suggested that each child pair off with an adult

THANKSGIVING TELEGRAM

1. Each player or pair gets paper and pencil.
2. Select a word with about nine or ten letters. Each player or pair writes the selected word at the top of his paper.
3. Make up a funny telegram by starting each of your words with the letters of the selected word using the letters in order. For example: MAY-FLOWER—*Mary Always Yells. Finally Louis Overturns Wheelbarrow Ending Riot.* Or, CRANBERRY—*Christopher Rests And Nellie Borrows Eddie's Red Rider Yoyo.*
4. Read telegrams aloud.

REVERSE THE POP CORN

1. Each player or pair gets ten pieces of pop corn.
2. Have them shape pop corn into triangle shown.

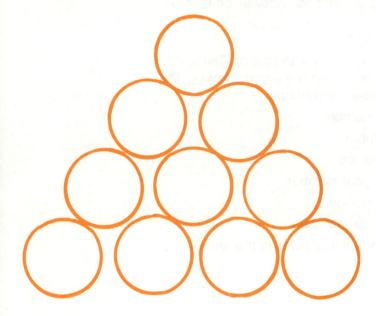

3. The object of the game is to reverse the triangle in only three moves. Only one piece of pop corn can be moved at one time.
4. Set a time limit. Answer on p. 142.

THREE INTO FOUR

1. You'll need three straight objects such as three straws, rulers, spoons or sticks.
2. The object of the game is to make three into four without cutting or bending. Answer on p. 142.

IT'S ALWAYS THREE

Give each player or pair pencil and paper. Tell them, "I can make all of you have the same answer. Do this." Then give these instructions:

1. Write down any number.
2. Double your number.
3. Add 9 to your number.
4. Subtract 3 from your number.
5. Divide your number by 2.
6. Subtract your original number.
7. Now tell everyone their answer is the same! It's always "3."

MIND READING

Mind reading has always fascinated people. Let your guests have a crack at it.

1. Give each player a piece of paper with a column of numbers from 1 to 20 written down the side.

2. From a regular deck of cards remove all of the cards except the 2s, 3s, 4s, 5s and 6s. This will leave you with a pack of 20.

3. Select one person to be the card reader. He shuffles and places the pack face down on a table in front of himself.

4. He picks up the first card from the pack so the players cannot see it. He concentrates for a few seconds on the card's number. The suit does not matter.

5. The players try to read his mind and put their guesses next to number 1 on their paper.

6. He continues until all 20 cards have been guessed.

7. Then he picks up the 20 cards which he has kept in order and reads them to the players.

8. The player with the most correct guesses then becomes the card reader for the next round of the game.

CONCENTRATION

This game is fun for young and old alike and is so easy to play that a person who has never played cards before can enjoy it.

Number of Players: 2 or more

1. Cut the cards to see who goes first.

2. Player with the highest card lays out the cards face down in 13 rows with 4 cards in each row.

3. The object of the game is to turn up 2 cards at a time trying to get 2 alike. For instance, two 8s, two aces, two jacks, etc. Cards must be turned up in full view of all players.

4. First player turns up any 2 cards. If they match, player picks them up and lays the pair in front of himself. He then continues to pick until his two cards do not match. If they do not match, player returns them face down to their original position.

5. Player to the left then takes his turn.

6. As cards are turned up, try to remember which cards are where, so when it's your turn, you can turn up 2 cards that match. In the beginning finding matching cards is luck, but as the game progresses, matching the cards will depend on your memory and concentration.

7. The winner is the player who has the most pairs.

Important: Do not rearrange cards during the game.

PLAN AHEAD

1. Give each player or pair a piece of paper with the following words written at the top. (The papers can be prepared while the turkey is roasting.)

thera⁻	smra	tulpo
evsun	remyeur	epunten
purijet	tansur	suruna

2. The object of the game is to unscramble the letters to make nine sensible words.

3. You can give your players a clue by saying, "Who knows where we will be eating our Thanksgiving turkey next year. Maybe at one of these places!"

4. Set a time limit. Answer on p. 142.

JOLLY TIME POP CORN WORD GAME

1. Give each player or pair pencil and paper.

2. At top of paper have players write Jolly Time Pop Corn.

3. The object of the game is to make as many words as possible from the letters.

4. Set a time limit.

5. Scoring: 2 points for each two-letter word; 3 points for each three-letter word; 4 points for each four-letter word and so on.

Another interesting way for adults to entertain the children after the turkey dinner and the Thanksgiving games is to read aloud the following facts about pop corn. School children can amuse as well as inform their classmates, especially during a history class, with these little-known facts about pop corn.

• *In 1519, when Cortes invaded Mexico he saw pop corn for the first time when he came in contact with the Aztecs who called their pop corn momo-chitl. At fiesta time, to honor the gods who cared for fishermen, they scattered the momochitl before the gods. They (the gods) would be pleased when its contents burst and looked like a flower. To honor another god, the god of war, the Indian maidens placed the pop corn over their heads, like a garland of maize, which they called mumchitl.*

• *In 1612, the early French explorers around the Great Lakes region found that the Iroquois Indians popped their corn in a pottery vessel on top of heated sand. Then they made a soup out of it.*

• *In 1621, the English colonists were introduced to pop corn at the first Thanksgiving at Plymouth, Massachusetts, by Quadequina, brother of the Iroquois chief, Massasoit. Quadequina brought a deerskin bag of popped pop corn to the dinner as a gift. During the peace negotiations with the English colonists, the Indians would bring pop corn "snacks" as a token of good will.*

• *In 1650, the Peruvian Indians used pop corn as a confection. They called it piscancalla.*

• *In tombs on the east coast of Peru, researchers found grains of pop corn perhaps 1,000 years old. They were so well preserved that they would still pop. This discovery proved H.C. Smith's theory about storing and drying pop corn in cribs for better popping (see page 8).*

• *The oldest ears of pop corn, or corn that would pop, have been found by archeologists in Bat Cave in west central New Mexico. They are about 5,600 years old. Before this discovery it was thought that pop corn originated in Peru about 1,000 B.C.*

• *The word "corn" has been bandied about for centuries. The biblical reference to corn during the "seven years of plenty" most probably referred to barley.*

- *In Scotland and Ireland, the word "corn" most often means "oats."*

- *In England, when they speak of "corn" they mean "wheat."*

- *Pop corn, a true whole-grain cereal, provides the roughage needed in everyone's diet. It is surprisingly low in calories: one cup of unbuttered pop corn contains only 54 calories.*

RECIPES

BEST WAY TO POP JOLLY TIME POP CORN

Before you can make these delicious recipes here's how to make your pop corn tender, crisp and popping good.

1. Warm the popper, heavy pan or heavy skillet.

2. Let the oil get hot—about three minutes. Drop in several kernels. When they begin to spin in the hot oil, it's time to start popping.

3. Pour in enough kernels to cover the bottom of the pan.

4. Cover and shake gently. When you hear the last few pops, remove pan from heat and empty contents into a large, buttered bowl.

Now that you've learned how to pop it right, here are some additional flavorings to sprinkle on your pop corn: garlic salt, curry powder or chili powder, grated American or Parmesan cheese, French dressing, barbecue sauce, Worcestershire sauce and broken nut meats

RECIPE GUIDELINE

1/4 cup unpopped kernels yields about 5 cups popped corn

1/2 pint equals 1 cup

1 pint equals 2 cups

2 pints equal 1 quart

POP CORN BALLS WITH SUGAR GLAZE

Ingredients

Jolly Time Pop Corn—4 quarts unsalted, popped corn
3 cups sugar
3/4 cup water
1 1/2 teaspoons salt
Large dash cream of tartar
Food coloring (optional)

Utensils

3-quart saucepan
Large roasting pan
Long-handled wooden spoon
Potholders
Waxed paper
Candy thermometer (optional)

• *Note:* 1/4 cup unpopped kernels makes about 5 cups popped corn; 2 cups popped corn makes one 3''-diameter ball.

Food coloring: Glaze can be used clear or colored with food coloring. The four standard food colors are red, yellow, green and blue. You can mix them to make other colors. For instance, red and yellow make orange, green and blue make turquoise. If you mix the same amount of each color together you get brown. A small amount of red makes pink, a large amount makes red. A small amount of blue makes light blue, and a large amount makes dark blue. Experiment!

1. Pop the corn following directions on p. 117. Discard any unpopped kernels. Place popped corn in roasting pan and keep it warm in a 250° oven. (Syrup coats more evenly if pop corn is warm.)

2. Combine sugar, water, salt and cream of tartar in 3-quart saucepan. Cook uncovered over medium heat until sugar dissolves. Stir often with wooden spoon.

3. After sugar has dissolved, boil gently for about 15 minutes or until syrup has become thick and foamy. When it reaches 260° on candy thermometer, it is done.

4. If you don't have a candy thermometer, here's another way to tell when the syrup is ready. Drop a half teaspoon of syrup into a small bowl filled with cold water. Gather the syrup up with your finger tips and form it into a ball. If the ball is hard, the syrup is done. If the ball is still soft, continue boiling the syrup, testing it every 3 or 4 minutes, until it reaches the hard-ball stage.

5. Remove pan from heat. If you wish to color the syrup, now is the time to add food coloring. Pour in a few drops at a time and mix thoroughly.

6. Carefully pour hot syrup over the warm pop corn in the roasting pan. Mix in the syrup with wooden spoon until all corn is coated.

7. Place a large bowl of water near your work area. When pop corn has cooled enough to touch, dip hands into bowl of water and shape the corn into 3''-diameter balls. If you pack the balls lightly, they will be easier to eat. Continue dipping hands into water as you work to keep pop corn from sticking to them. You'll have to work fairly quickly. As the syrup cools, it becomes harder to mold. It might be a good idea to have a few helpers.

8. Place pop corn balls on waxed paper. Set aside until glaze has hardened.

POP CORN BALLS WITH MOLASSES GLAZE

Ingredients

Jolly Time Pop Corn—3 1/2 quarts lightly salted, popped corn
2 cups sugar
2 1/3 cups water
1 1/3 cups light molasses
2 teaspoons vinegar
1 1/2 teaspoons baking soda

Utensils

3-quart saucepan
Large roasting pan
Long-handled wooden spoon
Potholders
Waxed paper
Candy thermometer (optional)

• *Note:* 1/4 cup unpopped kernels makes about 5 cups popped corn; 2 cups popped corn makes one 3''-diameter ball.

1. Pop the corn following directions on p. 117. Discard any unpopped kernels. Salt it lightly and place popped corn in roasting pan. About 10 minutes before syrup is ready, set it in a 250° oven. (Syrup coats more evenly if pop corn is warm.)

2. Combine sugar, water, molasses and vinegar in 3-quart saucepan. Cook uncovered over medium heat until sugar dissolves. Stir often with wooden spoon.

3. After sugar has dissolved, boil gently for about 45 minutes or until syrup has become thick and foamy. When it reaches 250° on candy thermometer, it is done.

4. If you don't have a candy thermometer, here's another way to tell when the syrup is ready. Drop a half teaspoon of syrup into a small bowl filled with cold water. Gather the syrup up with your finger tips and form it into a ball. If the ball is hard, the syrup is done. If the ball is still soft, continue boiling the syrup, testing it every 5 or 7 minutes, until it has reached the hard-ball stage.

5. Remove pan from heat, add baking soda and mix thoroughly. (Baking soda makes the hot syrup bubble and fizz.)

6. Carefully pour hot syrup over the warm pop corn in the roasting pan. Mix in the syrup with wooden spoon until all corn is coated.

7. Place a large bowl of water near your work area. When pop corn has cooled enough to touch, dip hands into bowl of water and shape the corn into 3''-diameter balls. If you pack the balls lightly, they will be easier to eat. Continue dipping hands into water as you work to keep pop corn from sticking to them. You'll have to work fairly quickly. As the syrup cools, it becomes harder to mold. It might be a good idea to have a few helpers.

8. Place pop corn balls on waxed paper. Set aside until glaze has hardened.

BEEFY POP CORN

One 2 1/2-ounce jar dried beef, chopped
1/2 cup butter or margarine
3 quarts pop corn, unsalted

Cook dried beef in butter for about 3 minutes. Heat popped Jolly Time pop corn in 250°F oven. Pour beef and butter over pop corn and toss to mix. Serve immediately.

SPICY POP CORN

Mix together 1 teaspoon each of salt, curry powder; 1/2 teaspoon each of turmeric, ginger; pinch of cayenne pepper, 6 tablespoons of melted butter or margarine; toss with 6 cups of freshly popped corn. Serve warm.

GARLIC POP CORN

To 1/4 cup melted butter or margarine, mix 1 minced or mashed clove of garlic, 1 teaspoon paprika, or 2 tablespoons grated Parmesan cheese. Toss with 6 cups of pop corn. Salt to taste.

CHILI POP CORN

4 quarts popped corn
3 small dried red chilies
1 package (about 6 ounces) peanuts
6 tablespoons soft-type margarine
1 package (about 3 1/4 ounces) sunflower seeds
3/4 teaspoon of garlic salt

Keep popped corn hot and crisp in slow oven (250°F). Cook chilies and peanuts in margarine over low heat for five minutes. Remove chilies. Add sunflower seeds and pour this mixture over hot pop corn. Season with garlic salt.

BACON 'N CHEESE POP CORN

1 pound of bacon at room temperature
1/4 cup butter or margarine
3 quarts freshly popped corn, unsalted
1/4 cup grated Parmesan cheese

Separate bacon slices and place in single layer on a wire rack set over heavy foil (with turned up edges) or over a very shallow pan. Bake in hot (400°F) oven until brown and crisp, about 10 minutes. Place bacon on paper towels to drain. Break bacon slices into 1/2" pieces. Melt margarine and gently mix with freshly popped corn. Sprinkle with Parmesan cheese and mix. Add bacon and toss to distribute. Serve at once.

JOLLY TIME CHEESE SNACKS

2 quarts popped corn
1/2 cup butter or margarine
1/2 cup grated American or Parmesan cheese
1/2 teaspoon salt

Spread freshly popped corn in a flat pan; keep hot and crisp in oven. Melt butter and grated cheese and add salt. Pour mixture over corn. Stir until every kernel is cheese flavored.

TANGY POP CORN FOR SEASONED SNACKERS
Ingredients
  3 quarts popped corn, unsalted
  1/2 cup melted butter
  3 tablespoons seasoned salt

1. Heat popped corn in a 250°F oven if it has been popped earlier.

2. Pour melted butter over pop corn, tossing to mix. Continue to toss pop corn and sprinkle with seasoned salt.

Seasoned salt
  6 tablespoons salt
  2 teaspoons paprika
  1 teaspoon dry mustard
  1/2 teaspoon garlic salt
  1/2 teaspoon celery salt
  1/2 teaspoon thyme
  1/2 teaspoon marjoram
  1/2 teaspoon curry powder
  1/2 teaspoon dill weed

Combine all seasonings and blend in blender, or mix well. Keep in a covered jar. Makes 1/2 cup.

TUNA DIP WITH POP CORN

This could be fun for a child's party. Children like to pretend they are grown-up and what is more grown-up than a dip?

Ingredients in blender

    8 ounces canned, drained tuna
    4 tablespoons sour cream or evaporated milk
    2 teaspoons chopped chives
    2 teaspoons chopped parsley
    Dash of paprika
    Dash of red hot sauce (optional)
    Salt and pepper

1. Blend to desired consistency.
2. Place in bowl with unsalted pop corn around it for dipping. Flat toothpicks are recommended to protect children.

POP CORN, PEANUT BUTTER AND JELLY SANDWICHES

Ingredients

    2 quarts popped corn
    Light syrup
    Peanut butter
    Currant or cherry jelly

1. Drizzle syrup over corn and stir until uniformly coated.
2. Press a thin layer of corn into well-greased jelly-roll pan; allow to cool.
3. Cut into squares and spread half the slices with peanut butter and jelly; top with second slice.

FISH 'N POP
Ingredients
    8 cups popped corn, unsalted
    2 pounds fresh or frozen fish
    3 medium onions, sliced
    2 medium tomatoes, quartered
    4 chili peppers, sliced
    Salt and pepper
    Dash of cayenne pepper

1. Boil and flake fish.

2. In skillet, brown onions then add tomatoes and chili peppers. Season with salt and pepper.

3. Simmer for about 1/2 hour.

4. Add flaked fish, cover and heat.

5. Place on bed of popped corn and garnish platter with additional pop corn. Sprinkle cayenne pepper.
    Serves 4.

FISH AND POP CORN CASSEROLE
Ingredients
    4 cups popped corn, unsalted
    6 ounces cooked fish
    4 ounces sharp cheddar cheese, cut up
    1 medium green pepper, minced
    2 cups evaporated milk
    Salt, pepper, paprika

1. Combine all ingredients in casserole, except pop corn.

2. Mix lightly, then bake at 350°F for 30-35 minutes.

3. Cover mixture with pop corn and place under low broiler until pop corn is golden brown. Serve immediately.
    Serves 4.

ORIENTAL PARTY CHICKEN
Ingredients
1 recipe Baked Caramel Corn (see p. 137)
3 1/2 ounces slivered almonds
2 chickens
2 eggs
2 tablespoons milk
1 tablespoon cooking oil
1/4 cup butter
1/2 cup brown sugar
1/2 cup soy sauce
Flour

1. Prepare one recipe Baked Caramel Corn. (For saltier, Oriental flavor, substitute 1 1/2 teaspoons soy sauce for vanilla in syrup.) Add 3 1/2 ounces slivered almonds to pop corn.

2. Have butcher cut 2 chickens in bite-size pieces (breasts in sixths, legs and thighs in thirds, and wing parts in half.)

3. Preheat oven to 350°F. Beat together 2 eggs, 2 tablespoons milk, 1 tablespoon cooking oil. Dip chicken pieces in egg mixture; dredge in seasoned flour. Slightly brown in skillet until translucent.

4. Melt 1/4 cup butter in shallow baking dish; arrange chicken in single layer.

5. Combine 1/2 cup brown or natural sugar and 1/2 cup soy sauce. Brush chicken with half of the sauce.

6. Bake for 30 minutes; turn chicken, brush with remaining sauce. Bake another 30 minutes or till crisp, browned and tender.

7. Place chicken on large platter arranged with baked caramel corn. Garnish with maraschino cherry halves and parsley.
   Serves 8.

JOLLY TIME CHICKEN
Ingredients
    4 cups popped corn, unsalted
    1 cut up chicken
    1 can cream of chicken soup
    1 can cream of mushroom soup
    1 can cream of celery soup
    2 pounds string beans, partially cooked

1. In mixing bowl combine and blend all three cans of soup. Do not dilute.

2. In casserole place a few pieces of chicken, washed but unseasoned.

3. Spread a layer of string beans on top of chicken, then cover with soup mixture. Repeat process until chicken, string beans and soup are exhausted. Should yield 3 layers.

4. Place casserole in preheated oven at 350°F and cook for 1 hour. No need to baste or turn.

5. When casserole is finished, garnish top with pop corn. If desired, a few slivered almonds go nicely with the pop corn garnish.
   Serves 4.

JOLLY TIME POP CORN AND CHICKEN

Instead of the usual bed of rice—try pop corn. It's low in calories and high in food energy.

Ingredients

6 ounces leftover chicken (or turkey)
2 cups diced mushrooms, cooked or canned
8 tablespoons milk
1 envelope instant chicken broth
Flour to thicken
Salt, pepper or any seasoning you prefer

1. Place milk and chicken broth in double boiler over low heat.

2. Slowly add flour to desired consistency. Blend and season.

3. Add chicken and mushrooms. When entire mixture is hot, remove and place on bed of pop corn.
Serves 4.

POP CORN CANDY

Ingredients

4 1/2 cups popped corn, unsalted
1 cup miniature marshmallows
1 cup confectioners' sugar
4 tablespoons light corn syrup
1 tablespoon unsalted butter
1 tablespoon water
1/2 cup chocolate bits or gum drops

1. Put pop corn in large bowl.

2. Put marshmallows, sugar, corn syrup, butter and water into saucepan. Put saucepan over medium heat and bring to boil, stirring occasionally. When mixture boils, reduce flame to lowest possible point (don't forget to use an oven mitt or potholder) and keep stirring constantly until all the marshmallows have melted.

3. Pour the mixture from saucepan over the pop corn in the bowl. Shake bowl or stir lightly with a spoon until all pop corn is coated with the syrup. Let the mixture cool slightly until you can touch it. But don't let it get too cold or it will get too hard.

4. While mixture is still warm, pour it into baking pans. With your hands press chocolate pieces or gum drops into the surface of the candy mixture.

5. When the candy has cooled completely, cut into wedges, wrap wedges in plastic wrap and store in a box or jar at room temperature.

COLORED POP CORN BALLS
Ingredients
2 cups sugar

6-ounce can (3/4 cup) frozen fruit juice concen-
trate (grape, orange, limeade, lemonade, etc.)

6-ounce can (3/4 cup) water

1/2 cup light corn syrup

1 teaspoon vinegar

1/2 teaspoon salt

5 quarts unsalted popped corn

1. Combine all ingredients, except pop corn, in a heavy saucepan. Bring to a boil; lower heat and cook to 250°F on a candy thermometer. Mixture will bubble up in pan, so watch it to keep from boiling over.

2. Pour slowly onto hot pop corn and mix until well coated.

3. Let stand 5 minutes or until mixture can be easily formed into balls.

4. Butter hands and form into 3" balls.
Makes 18 balls.

POP CORN BALLS NO COOKING

Here is a variation of pop corn candy that requires no cooking.

Ingredients

1/3 cup light corn syrup
1/2 cup unsalted butter (1 stick)
1 teaspoon vanilla extract
4 1/2 cups confectioners' sugar
48 pieces popped corn

1. Place corn syrup, butter and vanilla extract into bowl. Soften butter a little before you start. Blend ingredients thoroughly with wooden spoon.

2. Add sugar gradually and knead dough with your *clean* hands until it is thoroughly blended.

3. Take enough dough to form a 3/4''-diameter ball. Press a piece of pop corn into the center of each ball.

4. Store at room temperature in a tightly closed container.

CHOCOLATE COVERED POP CORN
Ingredients
  1/4 cup unsalted butter, plus enough butter to grease cake pan

  1 1/2 cups semisweet chocolate bits

  4 cups of popped corn

1. Put butter and chocolate bits into a large saucepan. Set pan over very low heat and stir mixture constantly until it melts. Take pan off the flame.

2. Let cool slightly.

3. Add popped corn to mixture until completely covered.

4. Place mixture into greased 13" x 9" cake pan. Spread it out evenly in pan gently with your hand. Let cool completely.

5. When cool, cut into 2" squares and put pieces into a box with waxed paper between the layers.

6. Store at room temperature.

CHOCOLATE POP CORN PIE
Ingredients
    2 quarts popped corn
    Light glaze
    6-ounce package chocolate pudding and pie
        filling
    Whipped cream

1. Drizzle glaze over corn and stir until uniformly coated.
2. Press into a 9'' pie plate, building edges higher than plate edge; allow to cool.
3. Prepare pudding and pie filling according to package directions. Spoon into pop corn pie shell.
4. Garnish with whipped cream.
    Serves 6 to 8.

Variations: Butterscotch or banana cream.

POP CORN NUT LOG
Ingredients
    6 ounces (3/4 cup) unpopped corn
    1/4 pound butter or margarine
    1 cup (6-ounce package) semi-sweet chocolate chips
    10 1/2-ounce package miniature marshmallows
    2 cups Spanish peanuts
    2 cups chopped pecans or almonds

1. Pop the corn and place in a large bowl.
2. Melt margarine, chocolate and marshmallows together in top half of double boiler.
3. Pour melted chocolate sauce over popped corn, adding mixed nuts gradually. Mix thoroughly until entire mixture is coated with chocolate sauce.
4. Spoon mixture into half-gallon paper milk carton, packing tightly. Place in refrigerator for 1 hour.
5. Cut lengthwise along all four corners of carton and peel carton away. Slice and serve.

POP CORN BARS
Ingredients
- 3 quarts popped corn
- 1 cup sugar
- 1/3 cup white corn syrup
- 1/3 cup water
- 1/4 cup butter or margarine
- 3/4 teaspoon salt
- 3/4 teaspoon vanilla

1. Keep popped corn hot and crisp in slow oven (300°F).

2. Stir and cook sugar, syrup, water, butter and salt until sugar dissolves. Continue cooking without stirring (270°F) until mixture forms a brittle ball in cold water. Add vanilla and stir only enough to mix it through the hot syrup.

3. Place popped corn in large bowl and slowly pour syrup over pop corn, mixing well to coat every kernel.

4. Wet hands slightly. Transfer mixture into flat cake pan. Let stand until cooled. Transfer to cookie sheet and cut into bars with wet knife.

JOLLY KA-RUNCH!

Ingredients
2 quarts popped corn
1 cup pecans
1 cup almonds
1 1/3 cups sugar
1 cup margarine or butter
1/2 cup white syrup
1/2 teaspoon cream of tartar
1/2 teaspoon baking soda
1 teaspoon vanilla

1. Mix popped corn and nuts on cookie sheet.

2. Combine rest of ingredients, except soda and vanilla, and cook to hard-ball stage. Cooking time is short—about 5 minutes. Syrup is ready when small amount makes firm ball in cold water.

3. Remove from fire, add baking soda then vanilla. Pour over popped corn and nuts. Mix to coat well.

4. Spread out to dry. When cold, break apart and store in tightly-covered container.
Makes about 2 pounds.

BAKED CARAMEL CORN
Ingredients
    1 cup (2 sticks) butter or margarine
    2 cups firmly-packed brown sugar
    1/2 cup light or dark corn syrup
    1 teaspoon salt
    1/2 teaspoon baking soda
    1 teaspoon vanilla
    6 quarts popped corn

1. Melt butter; stir in brown sugar, corn syrup and salt. Bring to a boil stirring constantly. Boil without stirring for 5 minutes.

2. Remove from heat; stir in baking soda and vanilla. Gradually pour over popped corn, mixing well.

3. Turn into 2 large shallow baking pans. Bake in 250°F oven 1 hour, stirring every 15 minutes.

4. Remove from oven, cool completely. Break apart. Makes about 5 quarts of caramel corn.

CARAMEL CORN CLUSTERS
Ingredients
- 1 package of caramels (about 28)
- 1/4 cup of sugar
- 1/4 cup of water
- 2 quarts popped corn
- 1 cup peanuts

1. Combine caramels, sugar and water in saucepan. Cook over low heat, stirring constantly, until mixture is smooth and comes to a full boil; continue to stir constantly while mixture boils gently for 5 minutes.

2. Combine pop corn and peanuts in large baking pan. Pour caramel sauce over pop corn mixture and quickly toss, using two forks until pop corn and peanuts are well coated. Spread mixture on cookie sheets. Let stand until cold, then break into clusters.

CINNAMON-SUGAR POP CORN
Ingredients
- 1/2 cup sugar
- 1 tablespoon cinnamon
- 1/2 cup melted butter
- 3 quarts popped corn, unsalted

1. Combine sugar and cinnamon. Heat pop corn in a 250°F oven if it has been popped earlier.

2. Pour melted butter over pop corn, tossing to mix.

3. Sprinkle with sugar and cinnamon, tossing to mix.

Attention: Cannot be used for decorations.

LIGHT AND FAST POP CORN GLAZE
Ingredients
2 cups granulated sugar
1 cup light corn syrup
1 cup water
1/2 cup butter

1. Cook to 260°F (hard-ball stage).

2. Pour over pop corn and mix thoroughly.

The above recipe may be used in an infinite variety of combinations—with food coloring and food flavoring (lemon, maple, cinnamon, wintergreen, etc.), with nuts and candy, chocolate squares, fruits—all added after the syrup is cooked.

DARK AND FAST POP CORN GLAZE
Ingredients
3/4 cup molasses
1 1/2 cup light brown sugar (or 3/4 cup each white and dark brown sugar)
1 tablespoon vinegar
1/2 cup butter
1/2 teaspoon salt

1. Cook ingredients to 280°F (soft-crack stage), stirring frequently.

2. Pour over popped corn and mix thoroughly.

The coated pop corn may also be molded into shells —pie-shaped or basket-shaped (small or large) to hold ice cream, canned fruit pie fillings, candies and other treats.

HONEY POP CORN BALLS
Ingredients
3 quarts popped corn
1 1/2 cups sugar
1 cup honey
1/2 cup butter
2 tablespoons vinegar

1. Boil ingredients until they stick together in water (not very long).
2. Pour over popped corn and let set until cool enough to form in balls.

EASY AND FAST POP CORN CANDY

1. Grind popped corn in food chopper, using coarse blade, until you have 2 cups of ground pop corn.
2. Mix 1 cup brown sugar, 1 cup molasses, 1/2 cup butter or margarine in medium-size saucepan. Cook until small amount forms soft ball in cold water.
3. Add ground pop corn. Pour into buttered pan. When partially cool, cut into squares.

BAKED POP CORN CRUNCH
Ingredients
    1/2 cup butter
    1/2 cup brown sugar
    3 quarts popped corn, unsalted
    1 cup whole pecans or mixed nuts

1. Cream butter; add brown sugar and cream until fluffy.
2. Combine pop corn and pecans. Mix with creamed mixture.
3. Bake in a 350°F oven about 8 minutes or until crisp.

PARTY POP CORN
Ingredients
    2 cups miniature marshmallows
    1/3 to 1/2 cup melted butter or margarine
    3 quarts popped corn, unsalted
    3-ounce package of fruit-flavored gelatin

1. Combine marshmallows and melted butter. Pour over popped corn and mix well.
2. Sprinkle fruit gelatin over all and toss to mix.

Answers

CHRISTMAS:

page 53: Who Lives In The House? Santa Claus

THANKSGIVING:

page 108: Three Into Four: make roman numeral IV

page 107: Reverse the Pop Corn:
  #7 moves next to #2
  #10 moves next to #3
  #1 moves to bottom

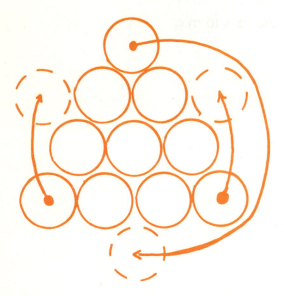

page 111: Plan Ahead: Earth, Venus, Jupiter, Mars, Mercury, Saturn, Pluto, Neptune, Uranus.

INDEX